Mentor Author, Mentor Texts

Short Texts, Craft Notes,
and Practical Classroom Uses

Mentor Author,
Mentor Texts

Ralph Fletcher

Heinemann
Portsmouth, NH

Heinemann
361 Hanover Street
Portsmouth, NH 03801–3912
www.heinemann.com

Offices and agents throughout the world

The author and publisher wish to thank those who have generously given permission to reprint borrowed material in this book:

"The Good Old Days," "The Family Plot," and "The Bravest Deed" from *Relatively Speaking: Poems About Family* by Ralph Fletcher. Copyright © 1999 by Ralph Fletcher. Reprinted by permission of Orchard Books, an imprint of Scholastic Inc., and Marian Reiner Literary Agency.

"Squished Squirrel Poem" from *A Writing Kind of Day* by Ralph Fletcher. Copyright © 2005 by Ralph Fletcher. Published by Boyds Mills Press. Reprinted by permission of the publisher.

Excerpt from *Spider Boy* by Ralph Fletcher. Copyright © 1997 by Ralph Fletcher. Reprinted by permission of Clarion Books, an imprint of Houghton Mifflin Harcourt Publishing Company. All rights reserved.

Hello, Harvest Moon by Ralph Fletcher. Text copyright © 2003 by Ralph Fletcher. Reprinted by permission of Clarion Books, an imprint of Houghton Mifflin Harcourt Publishing Company. All rights reserved.

Illustrations by Kate Kiesler from an early version of *Hello, Harvest Moon* by Ralph Fletcher. Copyright © by Kate Kiesler. Reprinted by permission of the illustrator.

Library of Congress Cataloging-in-Publication Data
Fletcher, Ralph J.
   Mentor author, mentor texts : short texts, craft notes, and practical classroom uses / Ralph Fletcher.
      p. cm.
   Includes bibliographical references.
   ISBN-13: 978-0-325-04089-9
   ISBN-10: 0-325-04089-3
   1. English language—Composition and exercises—Study and teaching (Elementary). 2. English language—Composition and exercises—Study and teaching (Middle school). 3. Creative writing (Elementary education). 4. Creative writing (Middle school). I. Title.
LB1576.F4766 2011
372.62'3—dc22
2011013715

Editor: Kate Montgomery
Production editor: Patricia Adams
Cover and interior design: Lisa Fowler
Typesetter: Gina Poirier
Manufacturing: Steve Bernier

Printed in the United States of America on acid-free paper
15 14 13 12 11 ML 1 2 3 4 5

Contents

TEXTS & *Writer's Notes*

🔊 *The speaker icon indicates that a recording of me reading the text is available online. See page 9 for access to these resources.*

Contents

Contents

Acknowledgments

Paul Crivelli, Kate Morris, and Suzanne Whaley are the first people I need to thank for helping me with this book. You guys are flat-out awesome. Thanks also to Sam Bennett and Zoe Ryder White. I am grateful to these fine educators for road-testing these mentor texts in the classroom.

Wendy Murray was my editor on this book during the crucial, early phase. During this time we had numerous conversations that helped me hone a vision for what this book might become. I am indebted to her.

It was a great pleasure to work with Kate Montgomery, editor extraordinaire. Kate encouraged me to be expansive in imagining something different from the typical professional book. Thanks also to the rest of the Heinemann team: Lisa Fowler, Patty Adams, and Eric Chalek.

I am grateful for my other editors—Lois Bridges, Ruth Katcher, Christy Ottaviano, Dinah Stevenson, and Philippa Stratton—from whom I have learned and continue to learn about what constitutes strong writing.

Thanks to Jen Allen, Ilyse Brainin, Max Brand, Melissa Browning, Jody Chang, Ann Marie Corgill, Jill Corcoran, Ruth Culham, Jan Furuta, Georgia Heard, Dar Hosta, Anna Lee Lum, Katy Mayo-Hudson, Nancy Johnson, Miki Maeshiro, George Pilling, Linda Rief, and JoAnn Wong-Kam.

Thanks, Lucy.

Every one of us should have a Franki Sibberson in our life—a smart, supportive friend who is always there to provide encouragement (plus a generous dollop of humor).

Dan Feigelson was a very helpful sounding board for this book, as he often is with my books. Sharon Hill, along with Dan and I, presented on mentor texts at NCTE. Both of these educators pushed my thinking on this idea. Kudos to Katie Wood Ray—I had several crucial conversations with her that helped me unlock the puzzle of this book.

Thanks to Carl Anderson, Drew Christie, Barry Lane, Mike McCormick, Martha Horn, Tom Romano, Frank Serafini, and Artie Voigt for friendship and lively conversation.

Thanks, Dad: you and Mom raised a family where words, books, and ideas were valued and treasured.

My wife JoAnn Portalupi reads just about everything that I read. She and I have had countless conversations about poems, novels, films, art exhibits, and architecture. How lucky I am to have a soul mate with whom I can continue to develop my aesthetic about what is true, and lasting, and beautiful in the world.

Ralph Fletcher
May 2011

Mentor Author, Mentor Texts

CONTAGIOUS
Magic

*I*n the early 1840s there was a carpenter in Brooklyn, New York, who worked framing two- and three-room houses. He had worked as a journalist and produced some unimpressive fiction. His literary career was not promising. But in 1855 this man shocked the world by publishing a collection of poems that immediately was recognized as a classic.

The book was *Leaves of Grass*. The man: Walt Whitman.

How could a virtually unknown writer come out of nowhere to produce such a work? It may have seemed sudden, but it turns out that in the 1840s Whitman had been undergoing a remarkable transformation, one sparked by reading the essays of Ralph Waldo Emerson.

"I was simmering, simmering, simmering," Whitman would famously say to John Townsend Trowbridge in 1860. "Emerson brought me to a boil."

Whitman seemed to be acknowledging that he could only go so far on his own. In order for him to fully tap his potential, Whitman had to apprentice himself to a writer such as Emerson. This story carries important implications for writing teachers.

Our students, too, are simmering, simmering, simmering. How can we connect them to their Emersons? How can we bring them to a boil?

Reading That Inspires Writing

Writing is slippery stuff. How does anyone learn to do it well? To enhance the development of their students, many writing teachers turn to high-quality examples crafted by skilled professionals. These texts have been called many things: models, exemplars, anchors, and, more recently, mentor texts. I have made wide use of them in my books on teaching writing, and in my own growth as a writer.

I am certain that reading particular novels, poems, and plays provided a catalyst that helped me grow into the writer I am today. But I am less sure about whether I learned specific lessons from particular texts. Upon reflection, I believe it was more a case of quality by association. Reading wonderful works by other writers (*The Ox-Bow Incident, Angle of Repose,* or a poem like "The Bear," by Galway Kinnell) made me dissatisfied with my writing. My drab sentences just didn't cut it anymore. It was clear I had to shed my old writing skin and grow a better one. I needed a writing makeover. I had to upgrade my prose.

Powerful writing seems to contain a magical essence, one we hope might somehow rub off on us. As a young writer I spent untold hours copying the stories of Ernest Hemingway, sentence by sentence, word by word. With my atrocious handwriting, this was tedious, painful work. It seems pretty silly now, but I was quite earnest. I was hoping that, somehow, the Hemingway magic might rub off on me.

Writing teachers do a similar thing. We share mentor texts by the likes of Cisneros, Rylant, or Christopher Paul Curtis, hoping that their sparkling sentences might lift the writing of our students, or at least provide scaffolding for them to build sturdier texts of their own. But, as any writing teacher knows, it's not always easy. It turns out that this magical essence is not so simple to extract. And once extracted, it doesn't transfer easily to the student who reads it.

When it comes to fostering the reading-writing connection, we might imagine two ends of a continuum—teachers who do very little to connect young writers to exemplary texts, and teachers who do too much. There is a memorable Three Stooges cartoon in which Moe, Larry, and Curly get hired to work as chefs at a fancy restaurant. They each don chef's hats, sharpen their knives, and are eager to get started.

The first order arrives: "A bowl of chicken soup!"

"Coming right up!" Moe promises. He proceeds to pour some hot water through the carcass of a raw chicken, collects the water that comes out the other end in a bowl, and serves it to the unwary customer.

This is hilarious; everyone knows that such a cursory pass-through will not create much of a broth. But I wonder if we don't do something similar as writing teachers. We give students only the briefest encounter with a text, usually one of our own choosing. Then we lament the fact that their writing has not been richly flavored by what they merely skimmed.

At the other end of the continuum, we have teachers who make absolutely certain that their students have a sustained encounter with the specified mentor text. Kids are directed to copy excerpts in their writer's notebooks, answer a series of questions, reflect on what technique the author used, label it, and "write off the text" to produce similar texts of their own.

In this regard, we have drifted a long way from using provocative literature as inspiration. (To me, the phrase *anchor text* suggests something that weighs down rather than lifts up.) Consider what happens in a classroom when students are having trouble sitting on the rug and a teacher says: "I love the way Eliza is sitting so quietly and ready to listen." Typically, when one student (or one text) gets identified as a good example, it can create a great deal of resentment.

I once received an email from a middle school boy in Tennessee:

Dear Ralph Fletcher,

This year all we have done is use your books as anchor texts. All we've been doing is try to write like Ralph Fletcher. It hasn't been fun. To tell you the truth it's been wicked boring! Basically, you ruined 6th grade for me and the other kids in my class. Thanks a lot!

I was shocked to receive such a blunt, rude note. (I eventually did receive an apology from this student.) But his email disturbed me for another reason: I realized that it contained a nasty sliver of truth. My texts were being force-fed to him. He had been fletcherized, and he hated it. Who could blame him?

Open Source Mentor Texts

Part of the problem may lie in how we have approached mentor texts. Instead of moving from whole to part, we have gone in the other direction, beginning with a specific skill, strategy, or craft element and then looking for a text that illustrates that one thing. This runs the risk of reducing a complex and layered text to one craft element.

In this book I propose a new way we might look at these texts. To explain, I will briefly borrow the concepts of *open source* and *closed source* from the world of computer programming.

Closed source refers to software whose source code is kept a secret by its creators. This is done to maintain tight control over their system and to protect trade secrets. Microsoft Windows is closed source: nobody but the employees of Microsoft can read or modify its source code.

Are you with me so far? By contrast, *open source* refers to software whose source code is made available to the public. For example, Linux and Android (which are also operating systems, like Windows) are open source. Anyone can go read the code, see how they're implemented, and make improvements or copy the code for their own purposes. This creates a more democratic dynamic, allowing easier and more open access to users with programming skills. Talented users become co-creators, shaping the platform they are using. It's like one chef who keeps a prized recipe secret, as opposed to another who makes her recipe readily available for any would-be chef to use and tinker with.

All this computer talk makes me sound like I'm a computer expert, which I'm not! But I wonder: What would happen if we started thinking of mentor texts as open source? Instead of directing students to pay attention to this strategy or that technique, what if we invite them to *look at these texts and enter into them on their own terms.* This would give students more control, more ownership, and it would respect the transactional dynamic that is present whenever anybody reads anything.

Let's take a look at the following paragraph excerpted from "The Follower," a short story by Jack Gantos (*Guys Read*, edited by Jon Scieczka, p. 79).

I dislocated the fingers on my right hand, bruised the side of my face, and sprained my right shoulder. I limped home hunched over like Quasimodo and went straight to my room. A few minutes later I was barking in pain from relocating the joints in my fingers. I was so afraid my mother would see my bruised face that I stole my sister's makeup and powdered my bruise. At dinner I couldn't use my right arm. It hung limply at my side like an elephant's trunk. I must have pinched a nerve on contact with the ground that left my arm paralyzed. Perhaps for life. I ate with my left hand and food kept falling down my chin and shirt and onto my lap. (79)

If you read this aloud to students, or give them time to read it on their own, they will notice various elements in the text. Their connections will naturally range from the specific (the use of *barking* as a verb) to the general (the black humor of this piece). Here's one way to envision this range:

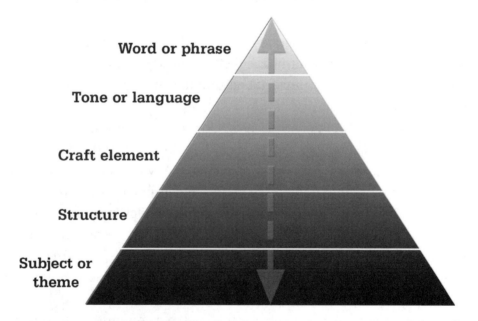

In this triangular schema, the most specific noticings (words, phrases, punctuation) can be found at the top; the most general (theme, subject) are represented at the bottom. I suggest that, in the democratic spirit of open source, we put students in charge of what they notice. Instead of directing students to pay attention to a particular strategy or craft element of our choosing, let's invite students to connect with *whatever aspect of the text they find the most intriguing or compelling*.

Usually when students look closely at a mentor text, we direct their attention to the *how* (the craft or the aesthetics of the writing) rather than the *what* (the subject or topic). But left to their own devices, students may not choose to connect this way. In fact, they may respond with questions or wonderings that pertain to the content:

- Is the narrator seriously hurt? Or is he just exaggerating?

- How come he doesn't want his mother to know the extent of his injuries?

- Quasimodo sounds like a funny name—who is he (or she) anyway?

Consider the issue of mentor texts in terms of watching a demonstration lesson in a classroom. Most of us have watched a teacher do such a lesson. Let's say that the teacher or staff developer asks observers to pay close attention to her writing conferences during the class. That's a worthy goal, but here's what is actually going on in the heads of the observing teachers:

Lucy is amazed by the high noise level in the classroom. She has never imagined allowing so much talk.

Karen is focused on one little boy who spends most of the period drawing instead of writing.

Dan is intrigued by the amount of writing displayed on the wall—not only finished pieces but lots of rough drafts as well.

Martha can't believe that the teacher is allowing students to write while sprawled on the floor (which isn't very clean).

It has been my experience that, no matter what I say ahead of time, observing teachers will focus on what they find most compelling. When I worked as a coach/staff developer, I found this to be frustrating, but I have come to accept that this is the way most people learn. *People focus on what they are ready to see.*

The same thing is true when we bring potent texts to young writers. I believe that when we give students a poem, story, or essay to read and respond to, they will zero in on what they are ready to notice. And that's okay. That's what I mean by open source. We can't control how students absorb these texts, nor should we. As writing teachers it is our job to find "stretch pieces," those rich texts that suggest new possibilities for students' writing. But let's honor whatever they notice, and use that as the building blocks of our teaching.

How to Use This Book

I wrote all twenty-four pieces in this book. You'll find an assortment of genres: stories, memoirs, poems, essays, picture books, and excerpts from novels. I tried to select short, high-interest pieces. Though some are taken from longer works, each one can also stand on its own with a beginning, middle, and ending. I tried to choose pieces that would bring a sense of closure by the end. The various texts have been arranged

. . . let's invite students to connect with whatever aspect of the text they find intriguing or compelling.

so that easier (less challenging) texts can be found at the beginning; more challenging texts can be found toward the end.

Some teachers will be inclined to assign particular texts for the entire class to read. There may be value in doing so on occasion, but as much as possible I'd prefer that you *invite* students to select those pieces from which they can learn. Realistically, your students probably will not love each and every one of these texts. That's okay. If they read one of these pieces and have trouble connecting to it, I would suggest they simply skip ahead to the next one.

"We're doing mentor texts," a teacher once told me. This comment made me cringe, but it also got me thinking. How do we structure close encounters between students and models from literature in a way that respects student autonomy and individual learning styles? Dick Allington has warned that too often we "do stuff" (activities, assignments, guided reflections, visual charts) with books. I worry that the same is true of mentor texts. Too often we direct students to "do stuff" with these texts, rather than allow them the choice and time to encounter the texts on their own terms.

So instead of assigning tasks for students to do with these texts, I suggest we offer them a range of strategies—we might even call them *approaches*—and encourage students to find the ones that feel right to them. In my introduction to students (see page 11), I put forth these suggestions:

- **Read at least once for pleasure.** The mentor texts we learn the most from, the ones that have the biggest impact on our own writing, are the pieces we truly enjoy.

- **Reread at least once for craft.** The first time we read for the what: content, ideas, and information. After we know what the piece is about, we can read it a second time for the *how:* craft. Robert Cohen, a novelist who teaches at Middlebury, once remarked to me: "I read everything twice, once to enjoy it, and once to steal everything I can from the writer."

  Rob is right—rereading is probably the most important way to delve deeper into the inner workings of a text and begin figuring out how the writer put it together. But it's a balancing act. As soon as we *require* students to undergo repeated rereadings of a text, we risk squeezing the life out of it.

- **Reread with pencil (or highlighter) in hand so you can mark up the text.** We want to encourage kids to be active, not stand back in awe or disinterest. Let's give them as much autonomy as possible in this regard; encourage them to make this process their own. For instance, instead of listing predetermined things for students to look for, you might invite them to come up with their

Sometimes it's enough simply to read the writing in a quiet place, to think deeply about it, and to let the words soak into you.

own labels for craft elements they notice. I visited a fifth-grade class where the students came up with various categories for things to mark when rereading a mentor text:

- *K & Q:* Keepers and quotables—parts you want to save verbatim just because you love the way they're written.
- *F:* Favorite parts.
- *CAT Scan:* Changes and transitions.
- *Whoa!:* Surprising words and phrases, or familiar words used in an unusual way.
- *Hello?:* Parts that don't make sense.
- *WE:* Writer's envy ("I wish I could do this in my writing!").

  It makes sense that students who create their own labels, and their own language, will take a more active part in rereading one of these texts.

- **Save texts (or snippets of texts) you especially like, maybe clipping snippets into your writer's notebook.**
- **Talk (in small-group or classroom discussions).**

In my introduction to students, in the spirit of anti-stuff, I add this: "It's okay to do nothing, too. Sometimes it's enough simply to read the writing in a quiet place, to think deeply about it, and to let the words soak into you."

After the kids have grappled with the mentor text in their own particular way, and possibly shared their noticings with each other, invite them to read my "Writer's Notes" section for that piece. Here I introduce the text, explain my thinking behind various decisions I made, and point out a few things I want kids to notice. With certain pieces, especially the last four, I highlight revisions I made along the way.

I could have gone on and on about each one of the pieces I wrote, but I made a point not to. I didn't want to squeeze the juice out of them. In his wonderful novel *The Sportswriter,* Richard Ford (1996) suggests that one danger in teaching is that *we talk the mystery out of our subjects.* Those words haunt me. As teachers, we risk talking the mystery out of good writing, something I tried hard *not* to do in this book. The writers' notes are not meant to be comprehensive. They are my way of opening the door and leading the student into the text. I did not attempt to make an exhaustive inventory of every craft element that might be found there.

Note: The writer's notes should not be played as a trump card or the correct answer given by an expert witness (me). It is my hope that the writer's notes can be included as another important voice—the author's insider perspective—in the discussion. Hopefully these notes will extend student thinking, not cut it off.

HOW TO ACCESS THE WHITEBOARD-READY MENTOR TEXTS AND AUDIO CLIPS OF RALPH READING HIS PIECES:

STEP 1
Go to
www.Heinemann.com

STEP 2
Click on "Login,"
to open or create
your account. Enter
your email address and
password or click
"Register" to set up
an account.

STEP 3
Enter keycode
MAMT-04089
and click "Register."

YOU'RE IN!

I suspect a book like this will raise as many questions as answers. As students read these pieces, I hope they will ask themselves:

- Is this mentor piece one I can learn from?

- What do I love? Or not love?

- What is this writer doing that I have never done in my writing?

- Why did the writer do this or that? What was his thinking in the decisions he made along the way?

- What seems most surprising here (in terms of how this is written)?

- What is one part that I admire? Or don't admire?

- Does this mentor text have any takeaways—something I can take/borrow/steal for my own writing? If so, what?

I have long subscribed to the belief that talk is the crucial ingredient in the learning dynamic.

I hope these mentor texts will spark discussion, among both small groups and the whole class. I have long subscribed to the belief that talk is *the* crucial ingredient in the learning dynamic. My most fervent wish is for these pieces to work as catalysts for some "grand conversations" as you and your students wrestle with the big questions: What is good writing? How can we all become better writers? These are questions writers never stop wrestling with because there are no final answers. But asking those questions will help them grow as writers.

Reading the essays of Ralph Waldo Emerson was a pivotal event in Walt Whitman's life, one that allowed him to make a quantum leap in his own writing. It helped Whitman find his voice, one that has influenced generations of poets thereafter. Our goal should be nothing less when we bring powerful texts to our students—to help each student find him- or herself as a writer. We do that best when we give them the time, space, and choice to enter into the lives of these texts on their own terms. I hope the mentor texts in this book will provide students with new possibilities and ideas for where they might go next—not to fletcherize them, but to help them tap their own individual genius, to help them grow into the writers only they can be.

BY WAY OF

Introducing Myself

(for Students)

Hi. I'm Ralph Fletcher, and I want to tell you a little about myself before we get rolling. I'm the oldest of nine kids. On the street where I grew up we had our nine, plus there was another family of Fletchers (no relation) down the street and they had ten kids. Nineteen Fletcher kids! On that street either you were a Fletcher, or you pretended you were one.

Let's see, what else should I tell you about myself? Well, I like baseball, hiking, campfires, mustard, funny movies, novels by Cormac McCarthy, Jackson Browne songs, basketball, babies when they're just learning how to walk, Hawaii, grilled fish, blueberry pie with vanilla ice cream, dark chocolate . . .

I like writing, too. In fact I *love* to write. A day without writing just doesn't feel complete. I have written forty books, half of them for teachers, the other half for kids. I have a special interest in helping young writers. That's why I wrote this book. I gathered the short texts for this collection in the hopes that they would fuel you on your journey to becoming a better writer.

Too often in school, books and poems get dissected like so many frog legs. That isn't necessarily bad—it can shine a spotlight on an important craft element (writing technique or strategy)—but it has its downside, too. It's sort of like taking apart an antique pocket watch to see how it works. When you're finished, instead of having a beautiful pocket watch that can accurately tell time, you end up with dozens of glittering little pieces spread out on a table. Worst of all, the watch's heart, its ticking pulse, has stopped beating.

I didn't want kids to dissect these stories and poems, to smash them to smithereens. I knew there had to be a better way! In college I had one professor who would begin the class by saying: "Let's *unpack* this poem. . . ." I like that word. That's what I want to do in this book—not to *dissect* these pieces with you but to gently *unpack* them. It's my hope that the discussions we'll have will take you deeper into these pieces and, in the process, inspire you to try things in your writing you've never tried before.

> In college I had one professor who would begin the class by saying: "Let's unpack this poem…." I like that word. That's what I want to do in this book—not to dissect these pieces with you but to gently unpack them.

These twenty-four pieces of writing were all created by me. A half dozen of them are what I call "slices of memoir." You'll find an assortment of other genres: poems, stories, excerpts from novels, nonfiction, picture books, and essays. The first few pieces are easiest to read and delve into; the mentor texts become a bit more challenging as you move through the book.

When choosing these pieces, I put a premium on brevity. I wanted "microtexts" short enough to be read in one sitting. I tried to select high-interest pieces. Realistically, however, you may not love each and every one of them. That's okay. If you read one of these pieces and have trouble connecting to it, feel free to skip ahead to the next one.

I strongly suggest that you read each one at least twice. Read it once to enjoy it, paying attention to what it's about. Then read it again, and try to read it as a writer. During this second reading, pay attention to *how* the piece is written: word choice, surprising imagery, transitions, details, the varying length of sentences, or whatever happens to strike your eye.

When you read one of these selections the second time around, make sure you have a pen in hand so you can underline or circle any parts you find noteworthy. Go for it—mark up my texts! Feel free to make notes in the margins, too. Mark up any parts you want, for instance:

- surprises (unexpected things in the piece)

- what puzzled you

- great words or phrases you'd like to use in your writing

- favorite sentences (quotables and keepers)

- connections (to other books, other pieces in this book, or your own life)

After you have read a particular piece a few times and marked it up, turn to the Writer's Notes section. In this section I unpack the piece you just read and try to give the inside scoop. How did I come to write that piece? What was I aiming for? What issues did I wrestle with? What questions are still unresolved in my mind? Writing involves making a hundred decisions, and I was there when I made those decisions so I can talk about each piece from the inside out. In the writer's notes I point out a few writerly moves I want you to be aware of. Maybe you'll like something I do and want to try in your own writing.

The Writer's Notes sections are not meant to be encyclopedic—in other words, I don't try to point out everything. Rather, I focus on what I consider the most important things. In some of the pieces, especially the last four, I share the revision process I went through in order to reach the final version.

I suspect that these pieces will raise more questions than answers. As you're reading and rereading, you might ask yourself:

- Is this mentor piece one I can learn from?

- What do I love? Or not love?

- What is this author doing that I have never done in my writing?

- Why did the writer do this or that? What was his thinking in the decisions he made along the way?

- What is one part that I admire? Or don't admire?

- What seems most surprising here (in terms of how this is written)?

- Does this mentor text have any takeaways—something I can take/borrow/steal for my own writing? If so, what?

Okay, so you have read and reread the piece, marked it up, and read the writer's notes. Now what? Here are a few things you might do next:

- Make a copy of the writing and put it in your writer's notebook.

- Copy a sentence or short section of the piece into your writer's notebook, maybe mentioning why you chose it.

- Share it with a friend, zooming in on one part or craft element you really liked.

- "Write off the text"—that is, create a piece of your own that is similar to the one I wrote.

You're in charge of your own learning. This applies to these texts. I would never direct anyone to do *all* the items on the previous list of suggestions. And I would only suggest you try one of these things if it makes sense to you as a writer.

It's okay to do nothing, too. Sometimes it's enough simply to read the writing in a quiet place, to think deeply about it, and let the words soak into you.

Becoming a strong writer isn't like winning *American Idol*; you don't make it overnight. Learning to write well is a lifelong journey. Everything you read will have an impact on making you into the writer you'll become. I will be happy if these stories, poems, and other pieces become part of your journey. The word *inspire* means "breathe in." I hope you will breathe in these pieces—their spirit as well as their craft—and allow them to lift your writing. Okay, now let's have some fun together!

Ralph Fletcher

TEXTS & *Writer's Notes*

of fresh apple cider,

, and follow the river up forest.

ot and we branch off through a stand of st

ppings, and bear tracks. Everything here

ur of walking Bo

hare our only ap

ost," my brother sig

trees have veins like my

shed skirts. Tons of tree

ind dies. Bobby jumps up.

can hear the river calling!"

ff he runs and finds the creek! It cu

e caressed by the sun. Now we

ch the wet place where

ug, dripping,

home

River Heart

Close to the moist bank of the creek, my little brother and I enter the forest. We hide a jug of fresh apple cider, wedged underwater between two mossy stones, and follow the river up forest.

Later it gets hot and we branch off through a stand of stunted pines, past deer droppings, and bear tracks. Everything here is dark and still. After an hour of walking Bobby gets tired, so we find an old log and sit down to share our only apple.

"We're lost," my brother sighs, and tries not to cry.

The trees have veins like my grandma's legs, hiding us under huge hushed skirts. Tons of tree trunks creak above us. All of a sudden the wind dies. Bobby jumps up.

"I can hear the river calling!"

Off he runs and finds the creek! It curves and hisses and glistens, a silver snake caressed by the sun. Now we can follow it, racing downstream until we reach the wet place where that jug of cider is still waiting for us. I lift out the jug, dripping, triumphant, an icy throbbing river heart. We drink it slowly walking home, and I feel the river in my bones.

Shaping the Story

Have you ever been lost? It can be really scary, even if you're only lost for a short time. I first wrote "River Heart" as a free verse poem and then decided to try writing it as a regular story. After comparing the two versions, I decided it sounded better as a story, so I kept it that way.

This story is fairly straightforward, but I do want to mention a few things. Notice the shape of the story. It begins with the two kids putting the jug of cider into the river; they return to that jug at the end. This circular structure can be found in a million tales, from *Hansel and Gretel* to *The Lord of the Rings*. The characters start in one place, go off and have an adventure (encountering danger, love, loss, battle, etc.), then return to that place (somehow transformed by the experience) at the end.

Most stories have three elements: characters, plot, and setting. When I wrote "River Heart," I wanted to include vivid details about the setting. The kids get lost, so I wanted to describe the forest in a way that made it sound ominous, to suggest the edge of danger.

Most people would say there are two characters in this story. Actually, I count three. By the end of the story, the river itself has become a kind of character, one with its own throbbing heart.

I always write with the eye and include details to help the reader picture what was going on. But in "River Heart" I also wrote with my ear. I paid a lot of attention to sound. For example, one sentence near the end contains a series of *s* sounds—*a silver snake caressed by the sun*—because I thought that would bring in the sound of the river itself.

Do you have a favorite sentence? My favorite is "The trees have veins like my grandma's legs, hiding us under huge hushed skirts."

The Good Old Days

Sometimes I remember
the good old days

sitting on the kitchen floor
with my brothers and sister

each on our own square
of cool linoleum.

I'm fresh from the bath,
wearing baseball pajamas.

Mom gives us each two cookies,
a glass of milk, a kiss goodnight.

I still can't imagine
anything better than that.

Poetry, Memoir, or Both?

This is a poem from my book *Relatively Speaking: Poems About Family*. As you can see, nothing dramatic happens here. This is a mood piece. My purpose was to convey a sense of peacefulness, of feeling loved. You might think of this poem as a "micromemoir" written in three parts:

1. The first two lines tell the reader: *I am going to look back and remember an important time in my life.*

2. The next four stanzas describe the memory itself.

3. The last two lines tell the reader: *Now that I'm back in the present, I will reflect on why this experience was important to me.*

If you like the idea behind this poem, I invite you to put on the "shirt" of this piece and try creating your own version. Feel free to borrow the first two lines. Then describe what the good old days were like in your life. If you like, you can end with the last two lines from my poem: "I still can't imagine / anything better than that."

When it comes time to write memoir, consider using poetry as the form to do so. A poem doesn't have to be very long, and it doesn't have to rhyme, but it can still pack a punch.

The Family Plot

Whenever we go visit
Grandma and Grandpa
we always have to visit
a certain old cemetery.

Dad slowly steers the car
past the granite gravestones
while me and my brother
crack jokes from the backseat.

The family plot is on a hill
overlooking a stone wall.
Nice view, my brother says.
Good drainage, I put in.

Dad turns to stare at us, hard.
Grandpa says: *I'll be buried
right next to my sweetheart*
and Grandma smiles at him.

There's room for us all, Mom says
and the cheery way she says it
makes it sound like we'll be
camping underneath the stars.

Different Point of View = Tension

"The Family Plot" is another selection from my book *Relatively Speaking: Poems About Family*. My wife's parents grew up in Barre, Vermont. Once we visited a cemetery in Barre that featured beautiful marble headstones carved by local Italian stonecutters. We drove around slowly, awed by the stunning stonework. At one point, my father-in-law stopped the car and pointed to a shaded area beneath a large maple. He explained that he and his wife would be buried side by side on that very spot.

"I hope you don't crowd me, Rita," he joked.

We all laughed.

This sparked the idea for "The Family Plot," but I didn't write this poem immediately. In fact, I forgot about it. Years later the idea resurfaced and I decided to take a whack at it. I think what makes this poem work is the tension between the three generations and the friction created by their different points of view:

• The grandparents are almost nostalgic about visiting their final resting place.

• The parents want this to be a nice family outing, so they try to keep things upbeat and positive.

• The two brothers think the whole scene is bizarre. They deal with the situation the way kids often do, by making irreverent jokes about it.

I love to use puns and double meanings in my writing, which is why I chose to use the word *plot* in the title.

In the second stanza you probably noticed an example of alliteration (*granite gravestones*) followed by these two lines:

> *while me and my brother*
> *crack jokes from the back seat.*

Grammatically, this is incorrect—it should be written as "while my brother and I," but I decided to deliberately break the rules of grammar. I wanted to create a believable voice that reflects the way kids sound when they talk. It seems to me that most kids would say "while me and my brother" even if it's technically wrong. So I wrote it that way.

Most poems are either funny or serious, one or the other. This poem has a combination of both. I love to find odd or unusual subjects for my poems. I was drawn to the idea of writing about a cemetery, and thought it would have appeal to young readers. Also, it was fun including snippets of dialogue in the poem.

Endings are important in poetry. I have to admit I really like this one—both funny and edgy at the same time. Sarcasm is one of those things you don't want to overdo in writing, but I think it works pretty well here.

Quilt

We move from Ocean Street to a house on Acorn Street. Dad said it would be bigger than our old house, and I guess it is, but the moment we move in it seems like every corner of every room is filled to bursting with all the stuff, smells, and sounds of our family.

Right now Dad is painting the walls in the upstairs hallway while my brothers and sisters are busy raising holy hell . . . the baby yelling and rattling the walls of the playpen . . . Jimmy cranking up the TV way too loud in the den . . . Johnny and Joey wrestling in the living room . . . Tommy chasing Elaine full-speed down the stairs . . . meanwhile I'm at the kitchen table trying to read a book . . .

Mom is in the kitchen, too, standing by the stove. I'm watching her. She's humming, keeping an eye on the baby, brewing coffee, making a double batch of Toll House cookies, browning meat for beef stew, all at the same time. We are pieces of unsewn cloth, wild and loud, blowing all over the place. She's busy making the quilt of our family, somehow, stitching us all together.

Playing with Ways to Stitch Together Sentences

This short memoir piece draws on a scene that happened many years ago. Instead of writing it in the past tense, I decided to use the present tense to make it feel like it is happening right now. Creating that feeling of immediacy and "now-ness" is important when you are writing memoir.

The first time I wrote this, I used separate sentences in the second paragraph:

Right now Dad is painting walls in the upstairs hallway. My brothers and sisters are busy raising holy hell. The baby is yelling and rattling the walls of the playpen. Jimmy has the TV cranked up way too loud in the den. Johnny and Joey are wrestling in the living room. Tommy is chasing Elaine full-speed down the stairs. Meanwhile I'm at the kitchen table trying to read a book.

How differently this paragraph reads when each of these sentences begins with a capital letter and ends with a period! But when I reread it that way, those separate sentences just didn't sound right. I wanted the writing to reflect the experience itself. By using ellipses (. . .), I was able to create sentences that had no beginning and no end. They collide with each other, very much the way my siblings crashed into each other.

The last paragraph ends with the central metaphor. When it's possible, I try to end with my strongest line, so that's what I did here.

Sibling Blanketry

Living in a big family with so many people can be pretty weird, too. Ever go to bed on a cold night with heat turned down and your room so cold you have to pile a bunch of blankets on top of you? While you lie there you mostly feel the flannel sheet and quilt right next to you. With the other blankets, the ones added last, your body doesn't notice whether those blankets are made of wool or cotton. All you know is that they're helping to keep you warm.

In a crazy way it feels like that, living in a family with so many kids: Nate, Cyn (short for Cynthia), Teddy, Brad, Josh. Nate is like my closest blanket. We're less than a year apart. We share a bedroom. The other kids are my sister and brothers, but Nate is my best friend. And then there's the baby, Josh. I was almost ten when he was born. He's okay, as babies go, but most of the time I don't pay much attention to him. He's like that last blanket piled on my bed just before I fall asleep.

—excerpt from *Fig Pudding* by Ralph Fletcher (Clarion, 1995)

Using an Extended Metaphor

This is an excerpt from my novel *Fig Pudding*. The narrator, Cliff, talks directly to the reader, explaining his thoughts on having so many younger siblings.

Although this is fiction, I'm drawing from my own experience here. Cliff is the oldest of six; I am the oldest of nine. I'm putting my own thoughts and insights into Cliff's head to deepen him as a character.

These two paragraphs draw on a blanket metaphor. It might be fun to think of what metaphor you could come up with to describe your place among your siblings as the oldest, youngest, middle, or only child in the family.

This excerpt speaks for itself. The only thing I want to mention is this: Some people make the mistake of thinking that only poets get to use a simile or metaphor. Wrong! Powerful tools like metaphor can be used in whatever genre (essay, nonfiction, play, how-to) you happen to be writing.

The Bravest Deed

I'm shopping with Mom
at the supermarket
and we see a woman
yelling at her kid
who looks about three or four.

    She grabs the girl's arm
    smacks her on the bottom
    BANG! BANG! BANG! BANG!
    about ten times, hard, then
    CRACK! across the girl's face.

The girl is screaming
and the lady gets ready
to smack her again
but all of a sudden Mom
sort of steps between them
and asks: *Is everything okay?*
You're having a hard time,
looks like. I remember . . .

Mom points at me, laughing,
actually calms the lady down,
with that girl still sniffling,
and me standing there hoping
no one will notice my
trembling hands.

Trying to Capture an Awkward Moment

"The Bravest Deed" is a poem from my book *Relatively Speaking: Poems About Family* (1999). Have you ever been at a department store and witnessed a parent spanking a child? I find those scenes disturbing though they certainly are not uncommon. In our culture we have an understanding that parents discipline their own children. It's an accepted practice that other adults stand back and don't interfere when this happens.

In this poem the narrator's mother violates that taboo, gets involved, and stops another mother from hitting her daughter. Talk about an uncomfortable moment!

In some ways this poem is like a very short story. I don't say much about the narrator, but I think of him or her as a kid who is about eleven or twelve.

In a story the sentence is the unit of thought, but in a poem the unit of thought consists of those words in a single line. With a free verse poem like this, every line should communicate one image or idea. I try not to pack more than one image into any one line.

Notice that the poem is written in the present tense. It seemed to me that writing it in the past tense ("we saw a woman . . .") would have made it more distant. Once again, I deliberately chose the present tense because I wanted it to feel immediate—as if it is happening right now.

When you think about it, spanking is pretty bizarre—parents striking their own children! I wanted to reveal the violence of spanking, so in the second stanza I included sounds: *BANG!* and *CRACK!*

In the third stanza the unthinkable happens—the narrator's mother moves her body between the other mother and that mother's child. Notice the line "sort of steps between them." This line has an awkward sound to it. But when I pictured this moment in my mind it seemed like it would be a very awkward moment—one mother interrupting another who was engaged in spanking her child. I wanted the wording of the line to reflect what was going on in the poem.

The final stanza contains four words that end with -*ing*: *sniffling, standing, hoping, trembling*. Take a look at the final three lines of the poem:

> *and me standing there hoping*
>
> *no one will notice my*
>
> *trembling hands.*

Why do you think the narrator's hands are trembling? Maybe the narrator . . .

- is worried about Mom's safety—after all, she has put herself in harm's way

- feels deeply embarrassed that Mom would do such a thing

- is worried that Mom might share some revealing story about the narrator

- remembers getting spanked by Mom in the past

These are just some of the possibilities. You may have your own interpretation for the narrator's trembling hands. The job of a poem is to capture a moment, not to explain it. I didn't want to explain too much here. Rather, I wanted to raise a question, and leave plenty of room for readers to enter the poem and make their own meanings.

My Father's Hands

While my father was talking I tried not to stare at his hands, which were bigger and darker than the rest of his body. It was as if a larger man's hands had been somehow grafted onto his arms. At CarWorks, where he worked, my father's hands got coated in every kind of oil, lubricant, transmission fluid, and engine grime you could imagine. After twenty years, all those greasy fluids had soaked into his skin. He used a special soap that washed off the filth, but only the topmost layer. You knew that the other stuff was still there just below the surface. His hands would never again be deep down clean.

—excerpt from *Also Known as Rowan Pohi* by Ralph Fletcher (Clarion, 2011)

Developing a Character by Describing One Physical Attribute

In this excerpt from my young adult novel *Also Known as Rowan Pohi*, I am trying to describe the father of the main character by focusing the reader's attention on one part of his body—in this case, his hands. It has been said that the eyes are the windows of the soul, but a similar thing is true of our hands. You can tell so much about a person by looking at the hands. Are they soft or calloused? Muscular or weak? Scarred or elegant?

In this novel, Bobby's father is a car mechanic so his hands come into contact with many kinds of oily liquids. It's worth mentioning that in this novel, the father has done a bad deed with those hands. The last sentence in the excerpt ("His hands would never again be deep down clean.") has a second, ominous meaning.

One of the hardest things in fiction is to make a character come alive in the mind of the reader. You might think you have to describe everything about the character; the good news is that you can be selective. You might try this the next time you're writing a piece of fiction or memoir. Choose one part of that person to describe—eyes, face, hair, mouth, feet—and see if you can reveal the character by describing in detail that single feature.

Squished Squirrel Poem

I wanted to write about
a squished squirrel
I saw on the road
near my house last week.

You can't write about
a squished squirrel,
my teacher said to me.
I mean, you just can't do it.

Write about an eagle
or a dolphin, he suggested.
Pick something noble
to lift the human spirit.

I tried, I really did. But I kept
coming back to that squished squirrel.
Did his wife send him out
to fetch some food or something?

There was blood, and guts,
but here's what really got me:
he had pretty dark eyes
and they glistened still.

You can't write a poem
about a squished squirrel,
my teacher insisted,
but I don't think that's true.

Anything Can Be a Subject for Writing

This is a poem from my collection *A Writing Kind of Day*. A squished squirrel on the road is a highly unlikely subject for a poem; I guess that's one reason I like it.

Naomi Shihab Nye wrote a wonderful poem titled "Valentine for Ernest Mann" (1990). There's a line in that poem: "Nothing was ugly just because the world said so" (144). I love that line! People might think that a squished squirrel is a horrible thing to write about, but it doesn't have to be. If there's any message in my poem it's this: You can write about *anything* at all that touches your heart.

Strong writing has tension. In this poem the teacher encourages the kid to write about dolphins or eagles, but the kid is drawn in a different direction. That tug-of-war creates the tension. The teacher is dead certain that you can't write a poem about roadkill, but by the end we have a poem about that very subject! That's an example of irony, when two things contradict each other.

Is the second-to-last stanza too disgusting? I figured that if I was going to write about a squished squirrel, well, I might as well describe it. Otherwise, it wouldn't be very realistic. (I hope you didn't just eat lunch!)

Driving at Night

There are eight kids in my family, so it's not easy to squeeze everybody into our car. Elaine sits in the front seat between Dad and Mom. In the middle seat there's Jim, Tom, and me, plus the baby (Kathy) on my lap. Bob, John, and Joe are crammed in the way back.

Night falls. The combination of darkness, lights, and a belly full of Grandma's food makes everybody drowsy. Soon the car falls quiet. Then Mom starts to sing. Elaine, Kathy, and I sing along with her, but it's much nicer to listen to Mom's voice.

> *I see the moon and the moon sees me*
> *The moon sees somebody I'd like to see*
> *Shine on the moon and shine on me*
> *And shine on the somebody I'd like to see*

Dad lights a cigarette, opens the window a crack to let out the smoke, and in that second sleep enters the car. I can actually feel it. I picture it as some kind of lazy snake, friendly and invisible, slithering in through the window. Moments later I feel it brush past my legs.

Next to me the little kids are talking with low voices.

The moon's following us. Look. No matter which way we turn, it's right behind us . . .

"See the moon?" I whisper to Kathy.

No answer. Her sweaty head has gone limp against my chest. When I peek around to look at her face, I can see that her eyes are closed. She's asleep.

Mom continues singing. Moon River. Tammy's in Love. The Wonder of You. She sings every word like it really matters.

No sound from the back seat. Swiveling around, I see that those kids are dozing, too. Three more gone! The sleep serpent is moving around the car, silent, restless. One by one every kid falls under the spell. I wonder who will be the next victim. On the other side of the car Jimmy is leaning against the door, motionless.

Then I realize that Mom has stopped singing. She's dozing, too.

The only ones left are Dad and me.

The only noise I can hear is breathing, soft and regular, like a lullaby you might hear someone singing in the distance. That sound comes from every corner of the car, seems to lift out of the seats themselves, and tries to come inside my head through my ears and heavy eyes. The car seems to be filling up with a sweet, fine mist, which I think must be baby dreams and little kid dreams and mother dreams all mixed together. From deep in my throat a yawn tries to come up, and I have to swallow it down.

Dad lights another cigarette and snaps on the radio.

"Is the Red Sox game on?" I ask, piping up so he'll know that I'm still awake.

"Let's see," he says, and starts fiddling with the dial.

As the driver Dad's got no choice—he has to stay awake. He's Ralph Fletcher, but I'm Ralph Fletcher, Jr. I'm his oldest son. And I'm determined to keep him company, to resist that sleep snake until we get home.

Using Personification

As one of nine kids, I rarely got to spend time alone with either one of my parents. Driving at night, when everybody except my father and I had fallen asleep, was one of those rare times when I had my father all to myself.

This text is a good example of personification: describing sleep as a snake that moves through the car claiming its "victims," one after another.

A piece like this has a smooth feel, like a polished stone, but it didn't start that way. I spent a lot of time tinkering with sentences, tweaking verbs, replacing one word with a better one, etc. I did eight or ten drafts until this piece had the sound and feel I was looking for. Look at the changes I made in the first paragraph alone.

> *There are*   *to squeeze*
> ~~*We've got*~~ *nine kids in my family, so it's not easy* ~~*getting*~~ *everybody*
>
>   *our*
> *into* ~~*the*~~ *car. Elaine sits in the front seat between Dad and Mom. In the*
>
>   *plus*
> *middle seat there's Jim, Tom, and me,* ~~*with*~~ *the baby (Kathy) on my lap.*
>
>   *crammed*   *way back*
> *Bob, John and Joe are* ~~*sitting*~~ *in the* ~~*back seat*~~*.*

Two notes on craft: I tried to use synonyms for the word *sleep* so I wouldn't keep using that word over and over again. Also, there are a number of long sentences in this piece. I tried to vary the rhythm by including short sentences every so often.

Maple Syrup Buckets

At the edge of Mr. Wells' woods
I count eighteen rusty buckets
hanging from maple trees.

In these parts it's a known fact
that Mr. Wells has never smiled
in fact never speaks at all

though he once explained to me
why it takes forty gallons of sap
to make a single gallon of syrup

which made me wonder if maybe
he requires forty hours of silence
to make a single hour of talk.

He keeps bees, too: succulent honey.
Strange that such a sour man should
produce all that sweetness.

—poem from *Ordinary Things: Poems from
a Walk in Early Spring* by Ralph Fletcher
(Atheneum, 1997)

Tinkering and Tweaking

This poem is from my book *Ordinary Things: Poems from a Walk in Early Spring*. I live in New Hampshire, which is a big state for making maple syrup. My kids' elementary school had a working "sugar shack." In the spring, students collected the sap and boiled it down.

Did you notice that there's hardly any punctuation in this poem? In my opinion, excess punctuation can clutter up a piece of writing, especially a poem. I didn't want to do that, so I left it out, and it seems to read fine without it.

The final stanza contains the word *succulent*. It always makes me happy when I can use one of my favorite words!

Note again the tension in this poem—a dour, unfriendly man who somehow manages to produce an abundance of ultrasweet honey and syrup. Go figure!

Learning to Catch with Uncle Daddy

When I was little I was the world's worst catcher. And I mean the worst! Mom's got videotapes showing me with a glove and a Red Sox hat. Uncle Daddy throws me the ball, and I miss it every time. But he taught me how to catch.

Here's how he did it. He stood in front of me holding a rubber ball. He held the ball so close to my glove it was no more than one inch away.

"There you go, Rivers," he said and threw the ball, dropping it really, into my glove.

"Willie Mays!" he yelled when I caught it. He always called out the names of his favorite players.

Then he moved back a tiny step, so he was holding the ball maybe a foot from my glove. He tossed the ball and I caught it.

"Roberto Clemente!" he called when I caught it. His face held nothing but pride. Now back another step.

"Carl Yaztremski!" he yelled when I caught it a third time.

The same thing every day. We started real close together and moved back from there. If I missed one, he'd just laugh and throw it again. I got better and better and pretty soon I didn't need to start out so close to him. Pretty soon we were playing catch like any other father and his kid.

—excerpt from *Uncle Daddy* by Ralph Fletcher (Henry Holt and Company, 2001)

Showing Emotion Through Movement and Action

This excerpt is taken from my novel *Uncle Daddy*, a story about a boy named Rivers whose father has abandoned the family. After that happens, Uncle Daddy (one of Mom's older relatives) moves into Rivers' house and assumes the father role.

Since this is an excerpt from a novel, most people would categorize it as fiction, but in some ways it's also a how-to piece. It shows exactly how Uncle Daddy went about teaching Rivers to catch.

Notice the structure of this piece. It starts with a little introduction in the first paragraph. Next we see a particular scene, a moment in space and time, showing Uncle Daddy teaching Rivers how to catch. The final paragraph is a conclusion. I deliberately repeated "pretty soon" to link the final two sentences. The last line includes the word *father*. I wanted readers to say to themselves: But Uncle Daddy isn't his real father, even if he's doing all the things a good father should do.

This is an emotional piece, but I don't show the boy's feelings. Do you think I should have? I figured it would be better to let the reader infer what Rivers is surely feeling—love, pride—rather than hit the reader over the head with those emotions.

Squirming Wizards of Recycling

Can you guess what kind of pet I have? Here are two hints. I have hundreds if not thousands of them. Plus, they make a valuable contribution to the world.

If you guessed honeybees, you would have been wrong. In fact, I have a colony of composting red worms. Because of them, I almost never have to throw away any spoiled or leftover food scraps from the table.

I have always been interested in transformation: how one thing can morph into something else. Once upon a time there were people known as *alchemists* who believed you could turn lead into gold. (An intriguing idea, even if it's not true.) I have a rock tumbler that can turn common stones into polished gems. So when I first heard about worm composting, I loved the idea that common food scraps could be magically transformed into a useful thing.

Here's how it works: Instead of throwing away that half-eaten piece of pizza or scraps from the salad bowl, you feed it to a colony of red worms. The worms eat that stuff and turn it into rich soil you can use in your garden or for houseplants.

To get started I purchased a batch of red worms for $30.00 from a company in California. They look like common earthworms, only smaller. I also bought a composter that had four stacking trays. There are holes in the bottom of each tray so the worms can migrate up or down depending on where the food is. Mine is called an Upwardly Mobile Composter, a name that still makes me smile. I mean, are these worms hoping to move into a richer neighborhood or something?

I followed the instructions and got the composter started by mixing a "coir" (fibers from the husk of a coconut) with some dirt plus shredded cardboard. Then I added the worms and gave them a moderate amount of food. The instructions cautioned against over-feeding.

It worked! Red worms are not picky eaters. They will devour almost everything you give them, but they especially love coffee grinds, cereal, French fries, greasy pizza cardboard, moldy bread, and slightly spoiled vegetables. You know the glossy ad fliers you find in Sunday newspapers? It turns out that this paper is covered with clay during the printing process, and worms go wild for it. Recently I shredded a pile of this paper and fed it to the worms as a treat, which prompted my youngest son to complain: "You treat those worms better than your kids!" That is entirely untrue, though I do bring the composter into the garage during the winter so they don't freeze in the icy New Hampshire air.

The red worms produce the "soil" by eating the food and passing it out the other end of their bodies. This probably sounds pretty gross, but the resulting stuff is fresh and rich. Trust me: there is no unpleasant smell at all. You end up with grade-A loam for all your plants and shrubs.

These composting red worms are awesome pets. Maybe you can't cuddle up with them in front of the TV like you can with a cat or dog, but these little critters require very little care. Best of all, they'll happily turn your leftover food into valuable soil. In this way, the worm-wizards of recycling make this world a better place.

Bringing Readers into an Unfamiliar World

This is an example of nonfiction writing—I'm teaching the reader about worm composting. But you could also classify it as how-to writing. Here I take the reader by the hand and lead him or her through the steps necessary to buy and sustain a colony of composting red worms. My purpose was to explain worm composting in a way that would be clear, and make it seem like anybody can do it—which they can!

I actually have come to learn a great deal about composting worms, but I kept reminding myself that readers would probably know very little. They would be wondering about many things. What are red worms? Where do you get them? How much do they cost? How do they eat? I wanted to make sure to answer these basic questions.

Notice that I used questions several times in this piece. I have found that questions are a great way to engage the reader. As much as possible, I tried to make the tone conversational in this piece of writing. Also, if possible, I always try to interject a little humor in my nonfiction writing. I did that here.

When We Ruled the World

The last day of camp. The place is named Camp Harrington but they should have called it Camp Bliss because the summer has been a total blast. There are six of us—me, Sammy, Mull, Pedro, Greg ("The Slug") and Trey—and we've become closer than brothers. But now it's over. *Terminado*, like Pedro would say. I know I won't see them again 'til next summer, and that's only if all six of us end up coming back to this camp. A very iffy if.

We roll our sleeping bags and pack up our stuff. Nobody talks. The parents can pick us up any time between 9 and 10 a.m., and we are just sitting around doing nothing, when all of a sudden Sammy, our fearless leader, leaps up to rally the troops.

"C'mon, you losers, let's do one more loop around the lake!"

So we jump on our bikes one final time, all six of us wearing flip-flops instead of shoes, and start peddling like we're cranked on steroids. Sammy is in the lead, singing the Coldplay tune that has been "the" song of the summer: *I hear Jerusalem bells a ringing . . . .*

He sings at the top of his lungs, like he's some kind of rock god. We're goofing, laughing, singing, swearing, flying round Kendall Lake, when out of the blue a Volvo appears.

It's the Mullherns' car. The car window slides down.

"Time to go," Mr. Mullhern tells Mull.

"But, Dad—"

"C'mon. We've got a long ride, and the traffic's going to be murder."

Bang! Just like that, Mull's gone.

We wave goodbye to him, but continue riding. Now it's only five of us. We pass the stretch of lake where we deliberately capsized our canoes a week earlier.

All of a sudden a blue Ford truck appears. Another direct hit: Pedro is gone, too! His dad puts his bike in the back of the truck. We can see Pedro waving adiós from inside the truck as they drive away.

And that's how it goes during that last bike ride. We have no defenses. The parents pick us off one by one, shrinking our patrol, until Sammy and me are the only ones left, peddling around the backside of the lake. The road rises up and we reach the one place where we can see practically the entire lake sparkling before us.

All of a sudden I can remember every single thing we've done this past month. The night we smuggled bags of gummy bears and Swedish Fish into our tent. The rainy afternoon we raided the neighboring Girl Scout camp and they snuck us into their cabin. The "tube steaks" we ate and ate until they almost made us sick. The time we detonated a football-sized hornet's nest hanging on a tree near the scout-master's tent.

Without warning, my eyes tear up. I swear I cannot see a single thing, and have to skid to a stop so I don't crash into a tree. Sammy rides ahead while I stand there drying my eyes with the bottom of my T-shirt. Then he stops and peers back at me curiously.

"What are you doing?"

"Got something in my eye," I mutter.

He rides back and pulls up next to me.

"C'mon, genius," he says softy. "We gotta get back before our parents come. I don't want to be the last one left riding—and you don't, either."

"True."

"Hey!" Pointing across the lake, Sammy swears loudly.

"What?" I said.

"That's our car!" he cries. "We're under attack! They're coming to get me!"

"C'mon," I said, jumping on my bike. "I've got your back. We've gotta make it back to base camp alive!"

Making Fiction Seem True

Goodbyes can be hard, especially after a month of bonding intensely with kids your age with no parents around.

I wanted to create the sense of a gang of six boys. Although I don't say it in the story, I imagined them as being in sixth or seventh grade. I thought it would bog down the piece if I took the time to develop each character. We only really get to know the narrator, Sammy, and Pedro. I trusted that if I gave readers some names for the other three, they could flesh out the characters in their minds.

A few other random things I hope you noticed:

- The short sentences and sentence fragments, especially at the beginning.

- The use of slang to make the dialogue sound more realistic.

- The flashback where the narrator remembers all the things they did that summer. I was trying to decide how many examples to include. I finally decided that three—the magic number—would be the right amount.

- The kids talk like they're in a war zone. From what I know about boys that age, and my own experience as a guy, I think many kids would feel too vulnerable to deal directly and honestly with emotions, as in: "I feel sad. I'm really going to miss you." The war talk is one indirect way of handling it. And it's also a way of showing connection between the kids.

Although this piece may seem and sound like memoir, it's actually a piece of fiction. That's one of my basic goals whenever I write fiction. The story may not be literally true, but I want it to feel "true" to the reader (I know kids like this; I've felt this way; yeah, this could really happen) in the larger sense. Author John Irving puts it like this: "a writer's job is to imagine everything so personally that the fiction is as vivid as our personal memories" (2000, 163). That's a tall order, but that's what I try to do when I write fiction.

Spider Romance

October 11

If spiders are such solitary creatures, how do the males and females ever find each other? I've been reading stuff on how tarantulas mate. Captive spiders in a small tank can't avoid each other, but in open wild spaces it must be much harder to find a mate.

Most male spiders wander more than females, so it's usually the males who find the females. They find a silk thread and they can tell right away if it was made by a female spider from their own species, and whether the female is ready to mate. If so, they follow that thread.

But finding a mate can be dangerous—especially for the male who is usually smaller and weaker than the female. Spiders are always ready to kill and eat any insect or small animal that comes within range. And they won't hesitate to eat each other.

When male spiders want to get together with female spiders they act in special ways to avoid being mistaken for just another juicy bug.

Some male spiders pluck the web of a female spider in a certain rhythm to let her know he's a friendly male who wants to mate.

The male of one species (*Xysticus*) protects himself during mating by tying the female to the ground with silken threads.

When a male nursery web spider thinks he has found Miss Right he captures a fly, wraps it up, and gives it to her. She unwraps and eats his present—this gives him just enough time to mate with her. And escape.

A male crab spider ties up a female spider and while she's still wrapped up he is able to mate with her safely. After he leaves, she unties herself.

Consider how the black widow got its name. The female allows the male to mate with her. And to show her appreciation she kills him. Eats him. This isn't some kind of morbid fairy tale: it's a scientific fact.

It's lucky that human girls aren't this dangerous. Or who knows—maybe they are.

—excerpt from *Spider Boy* by Ralph Fletcher (Clarion, 1997)

Weaving Nonfiction into Fiction

Ever since I was a little kid, spiders have fascinated me. That's one of the main reasons it was fun to write the book this passage came from. If I were one of those people who detest spiders, it would have been much harder to write *Spider Boy*.

The main character in this novel is Bobby, a seventh-grade kid who has just moved to town. He is obsessed with spiders, and keeps a journal to record interesting facts about them. "Spider Romance" is one of Bobby's entries in his journal. It comes just after Lucky, a girl Bobby has just met, gives him a surprise one night: a kiss. Thinking about how male and female spiders court each other is Bobby's roundabout way of thinking about Lucky.

Since this is taken from a novel, you might logically label this as fiction. But clearly it is also nonfiction, a slice of information writing embedded in the book. Fiction isn't just a work of the imagination. In order to write this book, I read nine different books about spiders. Since Bobby's spider journal is an ongoing feature of the book, I wanted to make sure his facts were accurate.

However, I knew it would be too boring if Bobby simply copied facts into his spider journal. As much as possible, I tried to write it using words a kid like Bobby might say. Also, I knew it would be important for the reader to see Bobby react to the information, as he does at the very end.

Big Boys Don't Cry

Ralph Joseph Fletcher: my name, my father's name, and my grandfather's name. My grandparents lived in a one-floor apartment in Fall River, Massachusetts. They raised eight kids in that tiny, two-bedroom place.

Grandpa was tall and skinny. He was a nonstop reader, and loved the chow mein made at a local Chinese restaurant. The fingers on his right hand were stained yellow from smoking two packs a day of unfiltered cigarettes.

Grandpa was a stern man who rarely smiled. He taught high school English, and I bet his students didn't get away with much in his class. My brothers and I were a little afraid of him. Whenever one of us got hurt while we were playing, and started to cry, Grandpa would bark:

"Stop that! Big boys don't cry."

One time we were visiting them in Fall River when my little brother Johnny tipped over a trash can in the driveway. He was barely seven, but Grandpa gave him a murderous look.

"Do that again," he warned, "I will cloud up and rain all over you!"

Johnny burst into tears.

"Cut it out," Grandpa ordered. "Big boys don't cry. Clean up this mess before you do anything else."

When Grandpa retired from teaching he and Grandma Maggie stayed in their Fall River apartment. We'd visit them a couple times a year, or they'd come visit us.

Then, in the fall of 1974, the worst thing in the world happened. My brother Bob got killed in a head-on car crash. He was a high school senior. I was 21 years old, and I knew my world would never be the same.

At the funeral home they had an "open casket" for family members only. Some of my siblings didn't want to go see the open casket, and I understood that. But I wanted to have one last look at my brother's face. I walked into the funeral home and found the right room. My grandfather, my father, and I stood beside the casket. Three Ralph Fletchers. All of us gazing down at the swollen face of the boy who used to be my brother. Or was he still? It hit me that he would always be my brother, even now that he was dead.

"Well, at least he looks like Bobby," Dad murmured. Which struck me as the most pointless thing I'd heard in my life.

I heard a choking sound and turned to see what it was. Grandpa. He was bent forward, beginning to sob.

"It's not fair." Tears spilled down his wrinkled face. "It's just not fair."

"It's okay," Dad said, putting his arm around his father. "It's okay, Dad."

Bearing Witness

It has been said that poetry tries to speak the unspeakable. A story like this attempts to do that, too. There is nothing more painful to a family than this kind of tragic death. When I wrote this story (it's really a memoir), I wasn't focused on what craft techniques or nifty strategies I might use. I wanted to tell this story as simply as possible. To bear witness. I tried to get out of the way of the material, to let it tell itself.

Since my grandfather is the one who cries at the end—one of the sad ironies in this piece—I knew it was important that the reader get to know him first, to make him come alive as a character. Otherwise, it wouldn't be nearly as powerful when he breaks down at the end. That's why in the first half of this piece I describe him physically, and show him interacting with my siblings and me.

The Fire Bug

Dad didn't smell sweet like Mum. He didn't talk much, either. But if Billy was good, Dad might give him a coin for his piggy bank and rub the top of his head.

There was a metal box in the back yard where Dad burned leaves and paper. He called it the incinerator. The incinerator was the cage where Fire lived. Fire was a pet, noisy and happy, jumping and dancing. Fire was a friend who always wanted to play. Billy helped Dad carry magazines and newspapers to Fire, who was always eager for a papery treat. No matter how much paper they brought, Fire would devour it. Fire never seemed to get enough to eat.

Stand back, Dad warned when they went to the incinerator. *Don't get too close.*

Most paper burned with a yellow-orange flame. Newspaper comics made the flames turn blue, or silver, or other beautiful colors. One day Billy was watching a lovely green flame when suddenly he noticed something that made his heart-rate kick up a beat.

A tiny lick of flame was leaking out the far side of the incinerator. Billy understood: Fire wanted out! It wanted to escape!

Trying to act casual, he wandered over for a closer look. The little flameling slipped under the wire and crawled from the incinerator—two inches, three inches, four . . . Slowly but steadily it moved toward the pile of newspaper that was stacked nearby.

Friends help friends, and Billy wanted to give Fire all the help he possibly could, but he had to do it in secret. Working carefully, taking care so that Dad wouldn't notice, he nudged a few scraps of paper in front of the escaping flame, creating a path for Fire to follow.

What do you think you're doing! Dad demanded.

Dad rushed over and stomped on the flame, extinguishing it. Then he knelt down and grabbed Billy by his arms.

Didn't I tell you Fire is dangerous? Didn't I?

Billy dropped his head, trying not to cry, but Dad lifted his chin and looked him straight in the eye.

You little fire bug!

In that moment Billy felt naked and revealed. There was no place to hide. Bursting into tears, he wrenched himself from Dad and ran inside the house. He threw himself on his bed, and gave himself over to wrenching sobs. Never in his life had he felt such searing shame. And the worst thing about it: he knew his father was right.

Creating a Dramatic Scene with a "Hot Spot"

This short excerpt is taken from *The Bluest Flame,* an unpublished novel of mine. Fire can be dangerous, but many kids are drawn to it. Dad's extreme reaction to Billy at the end of the story makes it seem like there is something seriously wrong with the boy. In fact, a heightened interest in fire is a natural thing. I'm convinced that the main reason my brother Tom joined the Boy Scouts was so he could light a campfire!

Danger can be a handy ingredient when you're writing a story, so fire is a natural thing to write about. A few things to note:

Billy is a little kid. While writing this piece, I tried to imagine the entire experience through the eyes of a six-year-old.

Because I wanted to make the fire a character with its own distinct personality, I decided to capitalize the *f* in *fire.* That way Fire and Billy would be on par with each other, almost equals.

It has been said that when a boy and his father climb a mountain, the real story isn't what happens *to* them, it's what happens *between* them. The real story here involves the dynamics between Billy and his father.

I think it's important to slow down the "hot spot" (the climax or crucial moment) in a story. In this piece several things happen one after another: Billy helps to feed the fire, notices the tiny flame, gets excited, watches it begin to escape, walks over, sneaks it paper, and so on. The crucial part—when Billy is trying to help the flame escape—contains the most tension. I didn't want to rush through this part of the story. Instead, I tried to let it unfold gradually.

Stalking the Enemy

It has been said that a person's strength is also their weakness, two sides of the same coin. Elvis Presley and Michael Jackson were phenomenal performers but, like Icarus, they flew too close to the sun. In the end they became performers in their own lives. The bright lights of celebrity melted their gaudy wings.

I'm no Elvis but I realize that this holds true in my life. My strength is also my weakness. I am an impulsive person. The dictionary defines this word as "not thinking something all the way through." This part of my character has gotten me into trouble, for instance, when I was four and thought my crayons felt too cold so I put them on a radiator to warm them up. My parents were not amused to find rainbow streams of melted wax dripping down the radiator.

But being impulsive has its upside, too. I have never been afraid to reach for the golden ring. That's part of my personal philosophy. I believe that if you want something, you have to go get it, period.

When I think of the term "personal strength" there is one image that comes to my mind. I once read about a Native American tribe that had fearless warriors. These men had a unique and peculiar way of stalking their enemies. On noiseless feet they would sneak up close to their foes, shrinking the distance, moving closer and closer still, so close they could hear the sleeping breath of the enemy warrior . . . close enough to feel the heat of his blood. At this distance the warrior could easily kill his foe. Instead he reaches forward and taps his enemy on the shoulder. Then, before his "victim" realizes what just happened, the attacking warrior disappears into the forest. The message is clear: *I got to you. I could have ended your life, but I didn't. I had the stealth and the strength, but didn't have to use it.*

Imagine this from the victim's point of view. He is awoken from a sound sleep to find his mortal enemy touching him gently on the arm. What could be more shameful or demoralizing? After having their lives spared in this way, those warriors went home in shame and utter defeat.

This story made a lasting impression on me. It represents the kind of personal strength I admire most—having those powers available, but only using that power if forced to do so, when there is no other choice.

—excerpt from *Also Known as Rowan Pohi* by Ralph Fletcher (Clarion, 2011)

Including a Story or Anecdote in an Essay

This is an essay—a short piece of writing on a particular subject. I wrote this essay to answer the question: What personal strength do you have and how does it affect your life? You will find your own things to notice in this essay, but allow me to point out a few things:

- using an allusion to a myth in the first paragraph (Icarus)

- using a transition sentence—the first sentence in the second paragraph ("I'm no Elvis but I realize that this holds true in my life."), which links what preceded it with what will follow

- using examples to back up general statements (warming crayons on the radiator)

- breaking of the rules by using a run-on sentence: "On noiseless feet they would sneak up close to their foes . . ."—I deliberately made that sentence go on and on to build suspense

- using a striking example (how these Native American warriors defeated their enemy)

More than anything, though, I wanted to write a lively essay that would be interesting enough to engage a reader. That was my main goal.

Interview with a Coho Salmon

Q: Uh, excuse me, are you a salmon?

A: (puffing with exertion): Yeah.

Q: Could I ask you a few questions?

A: What are you, some kind of reporter?

Q: Sort of.

A: Well, okay, but make it quick. I'm beat. I'm on the final part of my journey, and I've still got miles to swim before I sleep.

Q: So what kind of salmon are you?

A: I'm a coho salmon. I live in the Northwest.

Q: Tell me about your life. Where did it start?

A: It started right here, in this stream, where my mother laid her eggs. I can't remember her—I was just a little egg back then—but sometimes I pretend I am talking to her. I call her "Sal-Mom." Get it?

Q: Very funny. So after you hatched, you became a baby salmon?

A: Yes. For the first year and a half of my life, I stayed in this stream. First I was an *alevin*. When I grew a little bigger, I was called *fry*. When I grew bigger still, I was called a *parr* or *fingerling*. I was just a few inches long then. After that I become a *smolt*.

Q: I always wondered: did you have to take swimming lessons when you were little? Is that a stupid question?

A: Yes, that is a stupid question. Baby fish don't take swimming lessons, silly. It's instinctual.

Q: Sorry. So what did you eat when you were little?

A: When I was an alevin, I lived off the yolk in my egg sac. After that I ate bugs, insect larvae, spiders, tasty stuff like that.

Q: Ugh, disgusting!

A: When I was about eighteen months old, I was ready to do something amazing. See, they call us salmon but they really should call us magicians. We perform magic tricks that no other creatures can do.

Q: (skeptically) Such as . . . ?

A: Until now I had been a fresh water fish, right? But then—presto chango!—I suddenly turned into a salt-water fish that could swim into the ocean! Salmon are *anadromous*. Hey, are you writing this down?

Q: Uh, sorry, right. Anadromous. How do you spell that?

A: A-n-a-d-r-o-m-o-u-s. That means we are born in fresh water, migrate to the ocean, and return to fresh water when we are ready to lay our eggs.

Q: Wow. That must feel weird to go from fresh water to salt water, huh?

A: Salmon are very adaptable. And that's no fish tale.

Q: (groaning) Okay, so then you swam out to the ocean.

A: The *Pacific* Ocean. C'mon, you must have heard of it! I spent five or six years in the Pacific, hanging out with friends. I was in terrific shape—I swam over a thousand miles. I really loved the ocean. I had a whale of a good time!

Q: (getting angry) Enough with the jokes! What did you eat while you were in the ocean?

A: The regular stuff: other fish, plankton, clams, the occasional squid. But then it was time for me to come home and lay eggs. And here's where I did my second magic trick. See, before we lay our eggs, salmon always return to the same stream where we were born. So I swam back here to this stream.

Q: Wait, I smell something fishy here. Let me get this straight. You leave your native stream and enter the ocean. You swim for a thousand miles all over the Pacific, for six years, but you still manage to find your way back to the same stream where you were born? Gimme a break!

A: (proudly) Go ahead and Google me. It's a fact.

Q: But how do you do it?

A: (smiling) A magician never reveals her secrets!

Q: (begging) Can't you give me a little hint?

A: Actually, nobody really knows for sure. Scientists think it might have to do with smell. Believe it or not, every stream has a particular scent. Some scientists think that maybe we can smell the stream where we were born. My sense of smell is very advanced. That's a nice deodorant you're wearing, by the way.

Q: Uh, thanks. By the way, how much do you weigh?

A: That's a very personal question! But what the heck, I'll tell you: twelve pounds.

Q: And now you're going upstream to lay your eggs?

A: Righto. My other coho buddies and I are all doing it together. When you have lots of salmon going upstream to spawn, that's called a salmon run.

Q: You must be hungry!

A: Actually, I've lost my appetite. I don't know why but I hardly eat at all when I'm swimming upstream. Weird, huh?

Q: What's it like to swim on an empty stomach?

A: Swimming upstream against this current for seven hundred miles? It's brutal! Not only that, but I've got to jump these fish ladders and, at the same time, dodge all kinds of vicious predators.

Q: (looking around nervously) Predators? What kind of predators?

A: Eagles. Hawks. And scarier creatures, too. Why, just around that last bend I got chased by a huge hungry grizzly. I "bearly" escaped. Swimming upstream can be "unbearable." A nice coho could get killed around here.

Q: Your bad jokes are killing me! But you've got me thinking . . .

A: What?

Q: Salmon are like living boomerangs. You start here, go out into the world, and come back to where you started.

A: Living boomerangs. Hey, I like that! I could use that for my obituary.

Q: (confused) Obituary? What are you talking about?

A: (quietly) I'm going to die soon.

Q: Oh no! When?

A: As soon as I spawn. I'll lay my eggs in a gravel nest that is called a *redd*. I'll deposit somewhere between 2,000 to 4,500 eggs. Hopefully I can find a strong male to fertilize them.

Q: Whoa, all those eggs will make a zillion coho babies!

A: No, they won't. Only a few of them will survive. I won't survive. A few weeks after I lay those eggs, my life will end.

Q: (sadly) Gee, I'm sorry to hear that.

A: Don't be. I don't have any tear ducts, but even if I did, I wouldn't shed any tears. After all, I'm a coho salmon, and I've had a great run.

Inventing a Character to Breathe Life into Nonfiction

"Interview with a Coho Salmon" is a piece of creative nonfiction. Obviously, you can't interview a fish, so this piece asks the reader to pretend. I'm trusting that the reader will be able to do so but, at the same time, I know that the reader needs to trust me. With a piece of creative nonfiction like this, there is an unspoken agreement between writer and reader that even if the piece is lively and funny, it will also be accurate. I can't invent fake "facts" about the coho salmon. It's got to be true.

My first task in writing this piece was to create the two characters: the interviewer (I imagine this person as me) and the coho salmon. I wanted to talk about spawning, so I decided to make the salmon a female. I didn't want to create a bland, generic salmon. Rather, I tried hard to create a particular character, a personality with quirks and attitude. This coho salmon is braggy and bossy. And she's not as funny as she thinks she is.

While writing this interview, I remembered a handy tip I have learned about nonfiction writing: "the power of one." It's hard for readers to imagine the countless carrier pigeons that were hunted to extinction, but if you write about one pigeon, the reader may be able to connect and empathize. The same thing is true here. There are millions of salmon, but I wanted the reader to get to know one of them.

I did a lot of research in writing this piece—books, a fishing magazine, numerous websites (including encyclopedias). I actually conducted a phone interview with a friend in Alaska who fishes for coho salmon. I tried to sift through all the information and to include the most important stuff. I deliberately did *not* include everything, for instance:

- how the female coho finds a mate
- what predators the coho must avoid in the open ocean
- the physical changes the salmon undergoes when it returns to the stream to spawn

I left out certain information I considered less important. Plus, I didn't want to overwhelm the reader with too much information.

You often find a specialized vocabulary in nonfiction writing, words like *parr*, *fingerling*, and *shedd*. I tried to set off these words by putting them in italics. And I made sure to explain these words so the reader would understand.

I included a few jokes and puns to make sure this piece wouldn't sound too boring to the reader. Finally, I tried hard to think of an easy-to-understand metaphor that would help readers envision the life cycle of the coho salmon. I thought of using a yo-yo, but finally decided that a boomerang would be better and more accurate since it travels a much farther distance.

Some people think nonfiction is boring, but it doesn't have to be. This interview was a ton of fun to write!

On the Back of the Bus

Jimmy Gonsalves was a small, wiry, smoke-skinned man who worked the fields in the neighborhood where I grew up. Word had it that Jimmy came from the tropics, maybe Honduras or Panama, though nobody really knew for sure. He was a familiar sight, wearing a straw hat to keep out the sun as he rode a tractor. The man was a gifted farmer. No wonder people were eager to hire him to work their fields.

"Run over to Jimmy's field and pick five ears of corn," my mother often said. We ran over, knowing Jimmy wouldn't mind, knowing there was no corn anywhere that was fresher or more delicious.

Jimmy rarely spoke, but he performed one feat that made him a legend among the neighborhood kids.

"Eat a worm, Jimmy!" we begged when we saw him.

On most days Jimmy would obligingly pick one up—not a little one, either—strip away the dirt with one hand, pop the wriggling creature in his mouth, and start to chew.

"Mmm," he'd say, smacking his lips.

We always knew what to expect, but every time we'd stand there, gaping in astonishment while Jimmy munched a big old earthworm.

During the school year Jimmy worked as a bus driver. His son Mark, who was my age, would be the only kid waiting on the bus when it rumbled up to my stop promptly at 7:55 in the morning.

One day I was sitting next to Mark in the back seat. There was another bus directly behind us, and as we were driving along Mark made some kind of gesture to the other driver. I never really knew what motion he made, whether it was friendly or rude or possibly misunderstood, but the driver took offense to it and started angrily beeping his horn. Jimmy had to pull our bus to the side of the road, and shut off the engine.

Moments later the other driver boarded our bus, and came barreling down the aisle toward where I was sitting. He grabbed Mark Gonsalves by the back of his shirt and pulled him off the bus. All the kids moved to the right side to see what would happen next. Through the windows we watched the driver yelling at Mark Gonsalves while Jimmy stood there, wiping his face with a cloth handkerchief.

Suddenly—OH!—the driver slapped Mark Gonsalves across the face, causing Mark's head to snap back.

Jimmy stood there, working his mouth, but said nothing.

Then it was over. The driver stomped back to his bus. Mark climbed onto our bus and took his seat next to me in the back. Without a word, Jimmy started up the engine and we lurched forward, continuing on the route to school. Out of consideration for Mark, I kept my eyes forward. After a few minutes I stole a glance at him. He wasn't crying, though this face was full of frustration and rage. I wondered who he was angriest at—the other driver for hitting him, or his father for letting it happen.

After a few minutes I realized my fists were clenched; later I would find a row of indentations where my fingernails had left marks on the palms of my hands. I knew I had just witnessed something terribly wrong, but I didn't know what to do about it. I felt ashamed at my own helplessness.

This happened in 1961, years before the Civil Rights movement began in the United States. Marshfield was a white town. Jimmy and Mark Gonsalves were the only people of color I knew. Many times I have thought back on what happened that day, and wondered if that driver would have dared to slap Mark Gonsalves in the face, with his father standing there watching, but for the color of their skin.

Re-creating a Disturbing Incident

Before this, I had never written about this disturbing incident. I have been hiding from myself—or avoiding it—for a long time. Finally I decided to take the plunge.

Before I started writing I interviewed my childhood friend Andy Hunt, my sister Elaine, and my brother Tom. I talked to them not because I doubted my memory, but because I hoped their memories might dredge up more of mine. Their recollections were very helpful.

As with "Big Boys Don't Cry," I deliberately tried not to use a lot of techniques or literary devices when I wrote this piece. I tried to tell the story in a direct, straight-ahead fashion.

In the first paragraph I knew it would be important to mention Jimmy was "smoke-skinned." This story is at least partly about race. I chose the title hoping it might remind readers of the famous incident involving Rosa Parks.

The part about Jimmy eating earthworms was fun to write—a juicy and disgusting detail—though I wonder if it pulls the reader in the wrong direction. A detail like that may signal the reader that this is going to be a lighthearted piece. In fact, the story becomes far more serious. I wasn't sure whether or not to cut it; finally, I decided to leave it in.

Time is a biggie whenever you write, but especially with memoir. When you write memoir you often end up using lots of habitual time. I do that here: "'Pick five ears of corn,' my mother often said." The word *often* tells the reader that this happened on a regular basis. There's an important switch when I focus in on the particular incident: "One day . . ." This ratchets up the drama and tension, and lets the reader know that we are entering an actual scene that only happened once.

In one sentence I use dashes to insert an interjection—OH! I wanted it to be like a gasp, to reflect the jarring impact of that slap.

I once read that a story "turns on a moment of silence." Note that when the other driver yells at and strikes his son, Jimmy remains silent. In some ways, that silence was the most terrible thing of all.

I have written ten or fifteen drafts of this story. In the earliest versions, something seemed to be missing. Rereading those drafts, I realized that while I had faithfully retold what had happened that day, I hadn't done enough to put myself into the story. In a good story, the narrator must be more than just a bystander. He or she should also be an active participant, a character in the story. In later revisions, I added a few lines to show my reaction (confusion, frustration, rage) to what had happened.

In the last paragraph I stand back from the actual incident to reflect on it, to put it in some kind of historical context. I believe that reflecting, looking back at an event with a new understanding, is an important part of memoir.

Seldom-See-Ums

The Rarest Insects on the Planet

Our planet contains all kinds of unusual insects: luna moths, stinkbugs, walking sticks, dragonflies, boll weevils, army ants. Now get ready to learn about a whole bunch of way cooler insects. Have you ever heard of a grub that makes maple syrup out of maple sap? A spider that steals webs from different kinds of spiders and stitches them together to make a web-quilt? A low-fat butterfly (called the *margerinefly*) that only sips low-calorie nectar? Hold onto your hat (and grab your bug spray) because awaaaaaaaaaay we go!

Meditating Mantis

This relative of the praying mantis crosses its legs as if in meditation. Although the praying mantis is a carnivorous insect, the meditating mantis is quite peaceful and gentle. A field of meditating mantises makes a distinctive sound: Ommmm . . .

Vampire Ladybug

Think all ladybugs are sweet and harmless? Well, think again! These ladybug look-alikes have the same red bodies and black spots as their famous counterparts, except they come equipped with ferocious fangs. A pack of vampire ladybugs has been known to drain the blood from a full-grown wild boar in a matter of minutes. (Also known as the draculabug.)

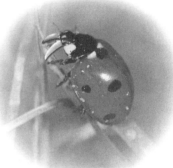

Math-Moth

Recently scientists were amazed to discover moths in Pago Pago, American Samoa, with actual numbers on their wings. A few rare ones have even been found with algebraic equations. Incredibly, they have never found any math-moths showing the wrong answer.

Quilting Spider

Spiders are famous for being sneaky, but this species has taken deviousness to a whole new level. This sly arachnid steals webs from other spiders to create dazzling "patchwork web-quilts" which are three times stronger than normal spider webs. These webs are perfect for catching giant Twinkieworms (a soft grub that measures exactly the size of one Twinkie when full-grown).

Tricerawasp

Most wasps have stingers on the back of their bodies. The tricerawasp's stingers are located in the front, very much like the horns of a triceratops dinosaur. If you are ever unlucky enough to stumble into a tricerawasp nest: run!

Santa Mantis

This fascinating member of the mantis family carries around a bag filled with wrapped "presents" (dead insects wrapped in dry grass) that it offers to unsuspecting prey. The moment the other insect begins to open the present, the Santa Mantis leaps forward and gobbles it up. Scientific name: *Hohohous sleighus*.

Gnap

This gnat spends its entire life dozing in the topmost branches of giant redwood trees, swaying in the breeze. Also known as the *dreambug*.

Ice Strider

This hardy bug lies dormant all summer and emerges in the dead of winter. It is identical to the common water strider except for one thing: the ice strider has "blades" on the bottom of its feet that allow it to skate gracefully on frozen rivers, lakes, and ponds. Some observers claim to have seen these creatures spontaneously divide into teams to play a version of bug-hockey, and do remarkable spins (including the triple axel) on the ice.

TV Fly

People bitten by this fly have been known to stare zombie-like for hours at a TV screen watching reruns of old *SpongeBob SquarePants* cartoons. The TV fly is a close relative of the dreaded tsetse fly except that it's smaller, has helicopter wings, and does not cause sleeping sickness. Wait, come to think of it, the TV fly is *NOTHING* like the tsetse fly!

Maple Syrub

This amber-colored grub lives in the mountains of New Hampshire where it can be found living in maple tree bark. This parasite drills into trees, sucks out the sap, and brings it back to its underground nest. There, other syrubs team up with symbiotic fireflies that heat the sap, evaporate excess water, and turn it into tasty syrup.

Rock Beatle

These blue-black beetles, which measure about one inch long, were discovered living in docks of Liverpool, England. Close up photographs show a face that bears a remarkable resemblance to a certain member of the famous band.

Sources

If You Give a Louse a Cookie (You'll Likely Lose Your Appetite), by Icahn C. Roachez, 2009, Varmint Publishers.
The Encyclopedia of Rare Insects Hardly Ever Seen by Humans, by Buz Fly, 2002, Critter Publications.
Bugged-Out Bugs, Scant Ants, and Other Tasty Dishes, by Harry Spydor, 2011, Web Media.
Unthinkable, Unheard-of, and Unimaginable Bugs, by Ivana Bugzapper, 2006, Cootie Books.
Crickets, Cicadas, and Other Annoyingly Loud Insects, by Juan Mohr Silence, 1999, Tranquility Press.

Making a Parody of an Insect Guidebook

I wanted to create a parody of a nonfiction guidebook, but I didn't want to make it too obvious that it was a spoof or satire. I wanted readers to take the book seriously, at least at first. My goal was to write it so that the truth would dawn on readers gradually: "Hey, wait a sec, this can't possibly be true!" Once they figure out that it's a piece of humor, they can still enjoy it in a different way, not as information but as pure entertainment.

Before I wrote this parody I did some research. I had never written a serious nature guidebook of this kind, so I spent time studying a number of published guidebooks of plants, mushrooms, rocks, and birds. I noticed that most scientific guidebooks contain certain elements and text features:

- catchy title
- introduction
- list of plants or animals (with the scientific name)
- sources
- diagrams, photographs, or illustrations

As I worked on "Seldom-See-Ums," I tried to include as many of these features as possible. Each one of these elements—even the "Sources" section—offered possibilities for humor. Since I'm not an illustrator, I didn't include any visuals, which would have made it much funnier. If such a book ever got published, it would be important to include mock-serious drawings and diagrams of each insect.

The narrator, the one who is "teaching" the information, is an important part of this piece. I deliberately included hints that would signal to readers that this narrator is unreliable and not telling the truth.

By the way, we have a pesky bug here in New Hampshire called the no-see-um. That insect gave me the idea for the title: "Seldom-See-Ums."

If I have learned anything from all my years of writing, it's this: Humor rules. Kids really want to laugh—grown-ups do, too! I giggled at least ten times while I was writing it, and that's a good sign. Usually if it's fun for me as a writer, it turns out to be fun for the reader, as well.

Note: I chose the final four texts because each of them required lots of revisions before it was finished. I thought it would be interesting to highlight all the changes I made, and share my thinking behind those changes along the way.

Beach School *(Draft One)*

Beach school has no desks,
no classrooms and no tests.

Sometimes we play at math
but we just do it for laughs.

No teachers teach;
no preachers preach.
No one makes a speech
if you reach for a peach.

But there's a ton of fun
plus the sea and the sun.
And I also should mention:
you can't get detention.

A New Kind of School

This is one of the pieces I wrote for "Summerstuff," an unpublished collection of summer poems. At one time or another all kids play school, so this is a universal topic that everyone can relate to. I thought it would be interesting to transport the idea of school to a beach setting.

To start, I wanted to describe beach school by emphasizing how different it is from regular school. So I listed things (desks, classrooms, tests) commonly found in any regular school that you would never find at beach school. You may have noticed that the first two couplets do not contain exact rhymes: *desks* and *tests*, *math* and *laugh*. These "off rhymes" are commonly used in poetry; I think they work pretty well here.

All four lines in the next stanza end in words that rhyme with each other. I wanted the tone to be playful and whimsical, though I realize it's not perfect. This stanza sounds a little *too* silly when I reread it now. And some of the lines don't make sense—for instance, what does a preacher have to do with school?

The last stanza ends on the word *detention*. I wanted to end on a word that captures the dark side of school: confinement, punishment. I figured that would be a great way to emphasize how dramatically different beach school would be.

Sometimes when I write something, I feel like it's not finished. There's more I want to say. The beach school idea intrigued me so much that I decided to try another draft of the poem. This time I decided to slow down and not limit myself to a tight rhyme scheme.

Beach School *(Draft Two)*

I draw a blackboard on the sand
using a shell as a piece of chalk.
I'll be the teacher, my sister the student.

Instead of a reliable school bell
we've got zany seagulls
cawing whenever they feel like it.

No desks, lunch count, or attendance.
There's no homework or detention.
It's okay to wear a hat in beach school.

No one cares if you run down the hallways
because there are no hallways.
Instead of regular school subjects we have
swimming, sunning, more swimming,
giggling, lazing, chip-chomping,
drizzle-sandcastle-making.

Nobody gets any grades or gold stars
though my sister finds a sand dollar
and I give her a starfish.

Recess goes on and on
forever and forever.

I write out a dozen difficult math problems
but the blackboard gets erased
by a wave.
Oh, well. No more math today!

Writer's Notes for *Beach School* *(Draft Two)*

Freeing the Verse from the Confines of Rhyme

The first version of this poem was *about* beach school. In writing this new draft, I decided to put myself into the poem as an actual character who plays school at the beach. That's a dramatically different way of looking at it. Putting myself into the poem gave me opportunities to try some new things.

As I began, I tried to envision the narrator. I pictured her as a girl around eleven years old, hanging out with her sister. So I had to see beach school through her eyes.

You might be thinking: "Whoa, hang on, Ralph Fletcher. You're a guy—why didn't you picture the narrator as a boy?" I don't know why. It just seemed more likely that girls would be the ones playing beach school, so I made the narrator a girl.

In this version I added more details to beach school, and some of it really feels like good stuff: wearing hats in beach school, the sand dollar, and so on. It was fun dreaming up various "subjects" the kids would "study" at beach school, like chip-chomping.

Any good piece of writing has to have an element of surprise. Whenever I write I try to highlight the unexpected, as I did with these lines:

but the blackboard gets erased
by a wave.

This revised version of the poem is definitely more detailed. The poem feels more intimate, too. I could imagine two kids actually playing beach school. But at the same time it feels looser and slacker. In some ways, the free verse poem version lacks the energy of the rhyming poem. It still didn't feel right.

What should I do now? I realized that it wasn't a matter of choosing between draft one and draft two. Instead I decided to go forward. As I reread the second draft a few times, I started to realize that it felt less and less like a poem. Maybe it was trying to morph into a new genre. Maybe it wanted to be a . . .

Picture book!

Suddenly I could see it: a picture book titled *Beach School*. Each page of text would be accompanied by sun-splashed illustrations. I didn't know if this would work, but I figured, what the heck, and decided to take a stab at it.

Beach School *(Draft Three)*

It's time for Beach School.   1
I'll be the teacher,
my sister Emily will be the student.

My brother Ray-Ray wants to play, too.   2
He's almost four-and-a-half,
plenty old enough for this school.

Emily takes a stick and draws a classroom in the sand.   3
In this school the walls are wide open
to let in lots of sun and breezy air.

I draw the blackboard   4
(we actually call it a sandboard)
and write the date and teacher's name:
Miss Periwinkle. (That's me.)

Instead of a morning bell we've got   5
zany seagulls crying **CAW! CAW!**
to get Beach School started.

It's my job to take attendance.   6
"Emily?"
"Here!" my sister says.
"Ray-Ray?"
"I'm hungry!" he yells. (He's *always* hungry.)

Ray-Ray digs a hole in the sand.   7
It fills with water as if by magic
and we study tiny creatures
darting this way and that.

I tell the class that baleen whales eat these tiny shrimp   8
which are actually called *krill*.
"I'm hungry as a whale!" Ray-Ray complains,
so I give him some crackers-with-peanut-butter.

Next we go on a field trip to a tide pool.   9
At Beach School you can't earn a gold star
but Emily does find a starfish, a real live one.

Ray-Ray likes the starfish so much   10
he invents a new song right on the spot:
"Twinkle, twinkle, little starfish . . ."

Later we lie on our backs to study the sky   11
and I ask what kind of clouds are floating overhead.
Emily knows the right answer: "Cirrus."
"Is it gonna rain?" asks Ray-Ray. He sounds worried.
"Nope," I tell him. "Cirrus clouds mean nice weather."

After awhile a golden retriever appears,   12
racing through one school wall
and out the other side.

"Hey, I almost forgot!" I yell. "Recess!"   13
We run off to ride the waves with boogie boards.

After that we do a science experiment   14
to see exactly how long it takes
to bury Ray-Ray in the sand:
five minutes and fifty-one seconds.

For lunch we eat submarine sandwiches,   15
watermelon, and salt water taffy for dessert.

Then Emily takes a turn being teacher.   16
Pretty soon she and I have changed places
so many times, teacher and student,
it's hard to remember who is who
and which is which.

Emily leads us on a scavenger hunt
and we find a long narrow shell.
I'm pretty sure it's a razor clam
though Ray-Ray calls it a *laser clam.*
"It shoots lasers at the bad guys!"
(Oh, brother . . .)

17

In the afternoon we have Silly Poem Writing Time:
> *Waves on the ocean,*
> *Waves on the sand,*
> *There's a monster waving at me*
> *With a seaweed-covered hand!*

18

But then—**OH NO! DISASTER!**

19

The entire sandboard gets erased
by a sneaky wave.

20

The tide is coming in—time to go home.

21

"Is there any homework?" Emily asks,
which makes us both burst out laughing.
That's one thing about Beach School:
there's NEVER any homework.

22

It's always a little sad to pack up and leave,
but I know we'll be back soon.
And Beach School will be waiting.

23

Creating a Picture Book But Still Thinking Poetry

In this draft I was focused on making a picture book with a beginning, a middle, and an end. But I didn't completely abandon the idea of poetry. A strong picture book (Jane Yolen's *Owl Moon* [1987], for instance) contains many elements of poetry: well-chosen details, wordplay, compressed language, and vivid descriptions. Those two genres have a lot in common. I wanted to make a picture book that would be playful, even humorous, but still infused with the flavor of poetry.

Draft two has a slower pace than draft one. In this third draft, I slowed the story down even further. I wanted a leisurely, unhurried pace. Timeless.

As I wrote each stanza I tried to imagine what illustration might accompany it. I never tell my illustrators what images to make. When they draw illustrations they respond to the manuscript, not to me. But I have found that getting an image in my head helps me to focus on what I want to write.

In this draft I added a new character: the little brother Ray-Ray. I pictured him as a pudgy little kid, belly hanging out, maybe wearing some kind of goofy sunhat. I figured that it wouldn't hurt to inject a comic element into this story. I tried to think of Ray-Ray doing and saying things that would make the reader laugh.

I decided to capitalize *Beach School* to make it more prominent and give it added importance.

I strongly believe that kids learn more by doing than by listening to a teacher talk. It hit me: if these kids went to Beach School, wouldn't they actually be learning things while they were having fun? I definitely didn't want to make the book too "teachy," but I decided to include a few doses of nonfiction. In this version, I added several stanzas that contained actual facts and accurate information: krill (stanza 8), cirrus clouds (stanza 11), and the razor clam (stanza 17).

In stanza 15, I deliberately chose three foods with a water/beach theme. I believe it's important to trust your readers. But, in this case, I have a nagging worry that they may not notice that. I wonder: should I have been more obvious?

Stanza 16 is my favorite. I'm trying to get across the idea that in any good classroom, students and teachers are both learning all the time. There's not a whole lot of difference between them.

This version still doesn't feel 100 percent finished. I've still got questions (Should I mention detention?), but I feel confident that the best form for this idea really is a picture book. That's the genre that gives me the necessary time and space to fully express what I'm trying to say, to let it grow and breathe. So I'm pretty sure I'm moving in the right direction.

The Old Baseball *(Draft One)*

Once there was a crisp new baseball, held together with 108 double stitches, and ready to roll.

The baseball would one day make it to the Major Leagues, but first it would play an important part in many little league games.

With this ball Shanetia Clark struck out the last batter of a game on her eleventh birthday. She pitched a no-hitter!

Another time a kid named Mike McCormick smoked this baseball to deep center, a home run that would have won the game, but the center fielder streaked back and speared the ball out of the air.

McCormick wept. Kids still talk about that catch.

During a night game this ball got hit into a high arc, an ordinary fly ball, except a curious bat fluttered down and tried to carry it off, thinking it might be something juicy to eat. The players thought that was so funny some of them fell down laughing.

This ball was used for many seasons. It was thrown and caught . . . bashed and battered . . . touched by a tear . . .

Over the years it got scratched and roughed up. A stitch ripped open. But the old ball stayed in the game.

One morning the baseball got hit into an oak tree, wedged in the V of a branch. The tree was too high to climb or poke with a long stick. Kids threw sticks and rocks, trying to dislodge it, but it was stuck tight. Finally they gave up and went away.

For eight days the ball stayed up in that tree, like a piece of unpicked fruit. Then a squall blew through town, bringing heavy rain and thrashing winds that knocked the ball loose and onto the ground.

Nobody knew it was there. Nobody claimed it. For three seasons the baseball had belonged to the Little League All-Stars. Now it belonged to the earth, the moon, and the stars.

During the next few weeks it got sniffed by a hungry doe . . .

. . . circumnavigated by an inchworm . . .

. . . clawed by a raccoon . . .

. . . who knocked it beneath a wild rhubarb plant where it stayed umpteen more weeks until a boy named Ethan happened to come along and pick it up.

Ethan studied the baseball. Once upon a time its coat must have been shiny white. Now it was darkened by dirt, stained green from grass. And heavy, too.

"Must be waterlogged from the rain," he thought.

He took a closer look. On one side a flap was torn open, almost inviting him in.

Ethan brought the ball home and showed it to his mother.

"It's nice you're giving it a new home," she said, "but what are you going to do with it?"

"I don't know," he told her. "Yet."

His big sister shrieked when she saw it.

"Germillion!"

"Huh?" Ethan said.

"Germillion means millions of germs!" she cried. "Throw that filthy thing away!"

"Not a chance," he told her.

Ethan showed the ball to his father. He lifted the torn flap.

"Look inside, Dad," he said. "It's filled with yarn."

Dad slowly rotated the ball in his hands. "Did you know that yarn is another word for story? This baseball must be chock-full of amazing stories! What are you going to do with it?"

"I don't know," Ethan replied. "Yet."

He brought the ball to his bedroom and stowed it under the bed. A week passed, then two weeks more. Every night he checked on the baseball before turning off the light.

On his birthday he got a new baseball glove which gave off a wonderful smell of fresh new leather. That smell gave Ethan an idea. He retrieved the baseball from under his bed.

"I know at least one more thing you can do," he whispered.

He nestled the old baseball in the pocket of his new glove. He wrapped the glove with three dozen rubber bands so the ball would stay snug and tight.

For added weight, he tucked the gloved ball between his mattress and box spring. It made his bed a little lumpy, but he didn't mind.

That night the ball stayed there, safe and undisturbed, like a seed in a protective cover. The old baseball would help form the pocket of Ethan's new glove.

That night, and all through the winter, they both slept soundly. And most nights they dreamed the same dream:

Ethan steps over the chalked baselines and runs onto the field with eight other players. It's the World Series! The stands are jammed with fans eager for the game to start. The umpire steps forward . . . brushes dirt off home plate . . . and cries out:

"PLAY BALL!"

The End

Writer's Notes for *The Old Baseball (Draft One)*

Keeping an Open Mind to a Revision Suggestion

In school, kids often get suggestions from their teachers as to how they might revise their writing. My editors do a similar thing, often giving me advice about what I might do to make my writing stronger, suggesting how I might recast or reimagine it in some way. Here is how one editor responded after reading *The Old Baseball*.

"I don't think *The Old Baseball* works as well as it might, although the idea is a good one," she said. "The story doesn't have much voice. It would work better, I think, if it were from the baseball's point of view. I bet it would read more rhythmically that way."

Hmm. That was my first reaction to this editor's suggestion.

Hmm.

That's *always* my first reaction. When an editor or someone I trust suggests how I might revise my writing, I try hard to keep an open mind and not reject it quickly. At the same time, I don't want to jump on the idea right away. I give myself time to think about it. It takes time for rainwater to percolate down through all the layers of grass, soil, subsoil, clay, and rock. It doesn't happen all at once. In a similar way, I try to be patient and allow time for a suggestion like this to work its way down through the layers of my consciousness.

Writing the story from the point of view of the baseball itself? Hmm. The more I thought about it, the more I realized that I . . . liked this idea! It gave me a new way to envision this picture book. In order to do what she suggested, the ball would have to be more than just the narrator telling the story. The old baseball would have to become an active character with a personality, attitudes, quirks, emotions, likes and dislikes.

Hmm. I also realized that if the ball were the one telling the story, it could now make little comments throughout the story. This might allow me to make the story funny (or at least funnier). With all this in mind, I decided to try a revision. Note the word *try*. I had not definitely decided to embrace this editor's suggestion. This new draft would be an experiment, a let's-see-what-might-happen-if-I-try-this-idea kind of draft. The following piece is what I came up with.

The Old Baseball *(Draft Two)*

Once upon a time I was a crisp new baseball. My leather skin was rubbed with New Jersey mud, and held together with 108 double stitches. I was ready to roll.

I played in more games than I could count, majors and minors, big and small. I got thrown and caught . . . bashed and battered . . . touched by a tear . . . clutched with a grin.

A girl named Shanetia Clark used me to strike out the last batter of a game on her eleventh birthday. With my help, she pitched a no-hitter!

Another time a boy named Mike McCormick smoked me to deep center, a home run that would have won the game, but the center fielder streaked back and plucked me out of the air. He held me up in the air like a trophy while the crowd roared. Kids still talk about that catch.

During a twilight game I got hit into a high arc, an ordinary fly ball, except a curious bat fluttered down and tried to carry me off, thinking I might be something juicy to eat. (That was scary!) All the players fell down laughing, so the umpire made us replay that pitch.

Over the years I got scratched and roughed up. Two of my stitches ripped open. But I stayed in the game.

One day a kid hit me into an oak tree where I got wedged in the V of a branch too high to climb or poke with a long pole. Kids threw sticks and rocks, trying to dislodge me, but I was stuck tight. Finally they gave up and went away.

For eight days I stayed up in there, feeling forgotten as a piece of unpicked fruit. Finally a squall blew through town, bringing heavy rain and thrashing winds that knocked me loose and onto the ground.

Nobody knew I was there. Nobody claimed me. For several seasons I had belonged to the Little League All-Stars. Now I belonged to the earth, the moon, and the stars.

During the next few weeks I got sniffed by a hungry doe . . .

. . . circumnavigated by an inchworm . . .

. . . tickled by a daddy longlegs . . .

. . . and clawed by a raccoon . . .

. . . who knocked me beneath a bush where I stayed umpteen more weeks until a boy happened to come along and pick me up.

"Hello, Mr. Baseball," he said. "My name is Ethan Paul."

How do you do? I silently replied.

Ethan studied me. I really needed a bath. My leather coat had once been shiny white. Now it was darkened by dirt and stained green from grass.

"You're kind of heavy, Mr. Baseball," the boy muttered.

(So, okay, yeah, maybe I had gained a little weight. Guess I was waterlogged from being left out in the rain.)

He gently touched the wound where my seams had torn open. "C'mon, old feller. You're coming with me."

Ethan brought me to his house. He showed me to his mother.

"What are you going to do with that dirty old ball?" she asked.

"I don't know . . ." he told her. "Yet."

When his big sister saw me she freaked and shrieked.

"Germillion!"

"Huh?" Ethan said.

"Germillion means millions of germs!" she cried. "Throw away that filthy thing!"

He shook his head. "Not a chance."

When Ethan showed me to his father, he lifted my torn flap.

"Look inside, Dad," he said. "It's filled with yarn."

Dad slowly turned me in his hands. The way he held me, I could tell he had played baseball before.

"Yarn is an old-fashioned word for story," Dad said. "This ball must be chock-full of stories. So what are you going to do with it?"

"I don't know . . ." Ethan replied. "Yet."

He brought me to his bedroom and stowed me under the bed. A week passed, then two weeks more. Every night he checked on me before turning off the light. I was happy to have a safe, dry place, but it was dusty under there. I missed the green grass and sunshine.

During those weeks I had lots of time to think. What was my future? Was I all washed up? Did I still have a place in the world?

Some nights Ethan would take me out and talk to me, using his softest voice so nobody could hear. I enjoyed those conversations. Often I would answer in my head.

"Hey, Mr. Baseball," he'd whisper, "did any pitcher ever throw a spitball with you?"

(Oh yeah, and lemme tell you, it was dis-GUS-ting!)

"Doesn't it hurt when you get smacked by a wooden bat?"

(Nope. That's what I was made for.)

"Do you miss being part of a real baseball game?"

(More than you'll ever know.)

On Ethan's birthday he got a new baseball glove that gave off a wonderful smell of fresh leather. All of a sudden he pulled me out from under his bed and tossed me into the air.

"I've got it, Mr. Baseball!" he cried. "I know one more job you can do."

First he nestled me in the pocket of his new glove. Then he wrapped the glove with rubber bands so I would stay snug and tight.

For added weight, he tucked the glove with me inside it between his mattress and box spring. It made Ethan's bed lumpy, but I guess he didn't mind.

That night I stayed there, safe and undisturbed, like a seed in a protective cover. I would help to form the pocket of Ethan's new glove. Could any job be more important?

That night, and all through the winter, I slept like a newborn baby. And every night I had the same dream:

The World Series! The stands are jammed with fans clapping and chanting, eager for the game to start. The umpire steps forward and brushes dirt off home plate.

"PLAY BALL!"

The first batter is Ethan Paul. He digs in and stares at the pitcher. Standing on the mound, the pitcher spits twice and takes a deep breath. Then he grips me, puts two fingers across my seams, and winds up to throw the first pitch.

I streak toward the plate, curving downward, but Ethan isn't fooled for a moment. He swings hard—**CRACK!**—striking me with the fat part of the bat. Then I'm off, rocketing in the opposite direction, heading toward the fences and making a whistling sound as I soar through the air. The crowd is going crazy, and I'm happy, too. Honestly, it doesn't hurt a bit when someone belts you for a home run. In fact, it has to be one of the best feelings in the world.

The End

Writer's Notes for *The Old Baseball (Draft Two)*

Switching to the First Person Point of View

I do like this new version a lot better. It's warmer, livelier, and more humorous. (It's funny how the baseball tries to claim some of the glory.) Because the old baseball has a personality, the piece does have more voice. Now that the ball is telling the story, giving us his perspective, I think readers will be better able to identify with him and his story.

Smoking *(Draft One)*

Mom and Dad smoked. Our house was filled with a thin, gray haze. That smoke was like some amniotic fluid in which we lived and breathed, not bad or good, just there, like the nonstop sound of kids talking, or the smell of cooking food.

Mom smoked while cleaning or washing dishes, especially when she was talking on the phone. When it rang she'd pick up—"Hi, Paulie!"—and cradle the receiver between her shoulder and cheek so her hands were free to unsheathe a cigarette and light up. Surrounded by babies, toddlers, noisy kids, she'd talk and smoke.

Dad smoked in the bathroom, in the car, at the kitchen table. He smoked at the beach, too. I loved the way he lit his cigarette at the beach when it was windy. He had a wonderful way of cupping a lit match against the wind, and bringing it to the unlit cigarette held between his lips. His face was never so fierce, concentrated, and alive as it was at that moment.

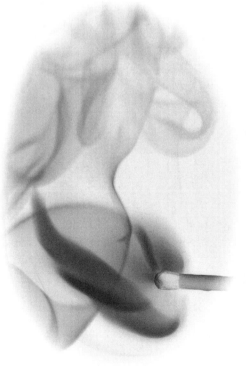

Writing a Draft That Feels Incomplete

A mirror reflects without judgment. I made a deliberate decision not to be judgmental in writing this piece. No matter what we might think of smoking today, it really was a big part of my life back in the 1950s and 1960s. I wanted this memoir slice to reflect that.

I think of a first draft like this as a "discovery draft." It's all about generating ideas, marking off my territory, finding out what I have to say, seeing if this topic truly interests me. When I reread this first draft I liked what I had written, but it didn't feel complete. I knew I had more to say, so I decided to take another swing at the piñata.

While revising this piece, I used a technique I learned from the writer Don Murray. Murray often talked about "layering." He described layering as going back and writing more about the subject, fleshing it out, incorporating additional memories, adding more ideas and details in order to thicken the stew. That's what I did. The next piece is what I came up with the second time around.

Smoking *(Draft Two)*

Nowadays many people consider smoking to be bad and unhealthy, but when I grew up smoking was "cool." Everybody smoked, and cigarette ads were every-where. We hummed along to catchy jingles on the radio: *Winston tastes good like a cigarette should.* We watched commercials for Kent, Kool, Marlboro, and Lucky Strike every night on TV.

In school the art teacher helped students make ashtrays out of papier-mâché. After the material hardened we would paint them, wrap them up, and proudly give them to Mom or Dad. My main Christmas present to my father was usually one of those papier-mâché ashtrays; he would beam broadly and hug me to his shirt (which always smelled like smoke).

My parents smoked Pall Mall regulars, unfiltered, and our house was filled with a thin, gray haze. That smoke was like some amniotic fluid in which we lived and breathed, not bad or good, just there, like the nonstop sound of kids talking, or the smell of cooking food.

Mom often enjoyed a cigarette while cleaning up the kitchen, but she especially liked to smoke while talking on the phone. When the phone rang she'd pick up— "Hi, Paulie!"—and cradle the receiver between her shoulder and cheek, freeing her hands to unsheathe a cigarette. Surrounded by babies, toddlers, noisy kids, piles of laundry and dirty dishes, she would talk and smoke, her eyes closed, leaning back against the wall. At those moments it seemed like the telephone cord and the smoke would coil together and form some kind of lifeline or umbilical cord that might magically transport her to another, calmer world.

Dad smoked everywhere: in the bathroom, in the car, and after finishing a meal at the kitchen table. I loved to watch him light his cigarette at the beach. He had a wonderful way of cupping a lit match against the wind as he brought it to the unlit cigarette he held between his lips. I thought his face never seemed so fierce, concentrated, and alive as it did at those moments.

Layering to Flesh Out Skimpy Writing

The first draft of "Smoking" contained 172 words. The final version is 340, almost exactly twice as long.

Since this piece is a personal memoir, you wouldn't think it would be necessary for me to do any research, but in fact I did. I went back to find out what were the most popular cigarette brands of that era. I think that listing them in the first paragraph—Kent, Marlboro, Lucky Strike—adds authority to this piece.

The second stanza was fun to write. I'm trying to inject some humor here. Of course nowadays it might be considered strange (or even rude) if a child gave a parent an ashtray as a Christmas present!

Interesting for me to realize that in the third paragraph I never use the term *second-hand smoke*. That's exactly what I'm talking about, but I thought using that modern term would dilute the memoir. We never called it second-hand smoke back then, so I deliberately left out those words.

Gesture (motions of hand or body to express an emotion) is one of the hardest things for a writer to communicate. In the last two paragraphs of this piece, I try to describe gestures my parents made while they were smoking.

Do you have a favorite sentence in this piece? I like the last sentence in the fourth paragraph, where my mother's cigarette smoke is compared to an umbilical cord. (This sentence didn't appear in the first draft.) This connects to the image of the amniotic fluid in the third paragraph. Building connections between various parts of a piece is a good way to create cohesion, so the writing feels like it holds together.

Note the small revisions in the final sentence. The first version reads: "His face was never so fierce, concentrated, and alive as it was at that moment."

The word *was* appears twice in that sentence. Nothing wrong with that word, but in general I try to avoid using passive verbs like *is* and *was*. By substituting active verbs, I made the revised sentence stronger: "I thought his face never seemed so fierce, concentrated, and alive as it did at those moments."

Creating **Hello, Harvest Moon**

It may seem that a published book materializes out of nowhere, dropped out of the sky. Not! You know all the decisions you have to make (who is the main character, how to start, what details to include, what happens in the middle, how will it end, and so forth) when you take a story from the initial idea all the way to publication. As a professional author, I am no different. Like you, I must make countless decisions, large and small, while I'm writing and revising a book.

Some years ago I took my third-grade son, Joseph, trick-or-treating. A huge moon had taken its place in the sky, making it easy to find our way from house to house. I realized we were bathed in the light of a four-in-one moon. It was a . . .

full moon

harvest moon

Halloween moon

blue moon (the second full moon in a month, which is rare)

That night I began thinking about the moon. It struck me that everybody likes the moon; it never puts anybody in a bad mood. The moon is our most accessible celestial body. If you take a baby outside on a sunny day, she's not going to point at the sun. It's way too bright. But babies love to point at the moon. In fact, *moon* is often one of the first words a baby learns to say.

So I did what I often do: I began writing about the moon in my writer's notebook. My entries are shown on the following page.

I wrote pages and pages like this. Some mornings I got up early so I could watch the moon setting in the sky. At other times I stayed up late, watching the moon, studying how the light changed when it dipped behind a passing cloud. I gathered, mused, speculated, and wrote many notebook entries. Coming out of a post office one day, I saw a woman wearing a shirt that showed a flower and the words:

Night-Blooming Cereus
They Bloom At Night

As soon as I saw that shirt, I thought: "Oh, I can use that."

I wrote and wrote for the next few weeks until I had ten or twelve pages of notebook entries. As I gathered these lines and images in my writer's notebook, an idea for a book began to take hold in my head. Maybe I could write a poetic picture book about the harvest moon, a book in the spirit of my book *Twilight Comes Twice* (1997).

So I started working on a manuscript. After two weeks I came up with the draft on page 85.

Something is stirring
   at the edge of the world
Something is rising
   low in the trees

The word <u>lunatic</u> comes from <u>lunar</u>

The moon climbs the night stairs
softly softly softly softly
walking on moccasin feet

          full
The ˅ moon rises
like a luminous balloon
tangled in far-away trees

moonshine, moonlight,
if you don't wear moonscreen
you'll get moonburned tonight!

The moon looks like the̶ ̶e̶y̶e̶ unblinking
of some god surveying our world

Native Americans had different names
f̶o̶r̶ the moon depending on the month
snowmoon (January)
hunger moon (February)
maple syrup moon (march)

My notebook entries

Hello, Harvest Moon *(Draft One)*

Something is stirring   1
at the edge of the world.
Something is rising
low in the trees.

It comes up round, ripe and huge   2
over autumn fields of corn and wheat.
Hello, harvest moon.

It lifts free of the treetops   3
and starts working its magic,
staining the sky with a ghostly glow
that blocks out most of the stars.

Like a celestial shortstop   4
it catches light thrown by the sun
and smoothly relays it to earth.

Wearing silent slippers   5
it climbs the night stairs,
pauses for a few seconds
over the house of Neil Armstrong,
and continues on its way.

The moon paints the wings of the owl   6
with a mixture of silver and shadow
that makes it hard to fly unseen.

It sends secret signals   7
to the eyes of solitary wolves.

If it had any feet   8
it would tap to the beat
of the dancing lunar moths.

In the desert it speaks to   9
the night-blooming cereus:
Now! Now!
and they open their blossoms.

A small boy in his bedroom   10
sees the man on the moon
and thinks of his father
before falling asleep.

A girl gazes up at the full moon,   11
a lantern for her new love.

The moon moves the earth's waters.   12

Grabbing whole oceans with its arms   13
the moon pulls in the high tide
that lifts all the boats,
        every row boat and yacht,
                tied snug at the dock.

It floods the clam flats   14
that were exposed in low tide

. . . and it floods us with memories   15
of every full moon we have ever seen.

It connects us to our distant ancestors,   16
those prehistoric women and men
who prayed to the harvest moon
yet feared it might be a god's
one unblinking eye.

Hours and hours later   17
it starts to ease lower . . .

. . . sprinkling silver coins   18
like a careless millionaire
over ponds, lakes, and seas,
til all the money is spent.

Look to the western horizon   19
if you want to see moonset:
a sleepy head
        falling
                in slow motion
                        onto its pillow.

Sweet dreams, harvest moon.   20

Using Feedback to Help Revise

I knew that this manuscript wasn't perfect, but I thought it was pretty solid. What happened next to me and my manuscript isn't very different from what happens to you. When you finish a piece of writing, you give it to your teacher, who makes suggestions about what does and doesn't work. My editor does a similar thing. She read the manuscript, and wrote me this letter:

I'm happy to have this submission, but I find Hello, Harvest Moon *in some ways a difficult piece.*

The idea of a moon poem as a kind of companion to Twilight Comes Twice *is exciting, and some of the images are lovely.* Hello, Harvest Moon *lacks the narrative motion of* Twilight, *however. And where* Twilight *offers the reader any number of connections to our everyday life and our sense impressions,* Hello, Harvest Moon *seems much more abstract. It's almost as though this poem is intended to include just about everything that anyone might associate with the moon (tides, young love, night blossoms, astronauts, wolves, folklore). The location keeps changing. The overall effect is more cerebral than in* Twilight, *and less immediate. It feels like a list of images instead of a story. I think it would have a greater appeal to children if there was a stronger narrative thread.*

Here are my thoughts about it, stanza by stanza.

Stanzas 1–2. The voice here is especially nice, with an almost childlike sense of wonder and magic.

Stanza 4. The shortstop image seems awkward to me. It is conceptual (a shortstop's role in baseball) rather than visual. It doesn't fit with the rest of the poem, and wouldn't be easy to illustrate.

Stanza 5. If the moon has no feet (stanza 8) how can it be wearing slippers? Also, kids won't have a clue who Neil Armstrong is, and it jars to have a real person's name mentioned in an otherwise nonspecific poem.

Stanza 6. I wish the third line referred more directly to the owl; the impersonal "it" is a stopper.

Stanza 7. But wolves aren't solitary, are they?

Stanza 8. Hard to follow. The moon doesn't seem to me to do anything like tap dancing, and luna moths are big and graceful and slow-moving, more like ballet dancers than tap dancers. Are luna moths still around in the fall?

Stanza 10. I like the simplicity and poignancy of the boy seeing the man in the moon and thinking of his father, but I find it too open-ended. Children, especially, will want to know what's happening here. Is the boy's father away? Is he dead? Or does the boy just happen to be thinking of his father, who is downstairs watching TV? I can't help stopping to puzzle over these questions, and that interrupts the flow.

Stanza 13. How come the moon has arms, but no feet? Also, if the moon grabs the ocean and pulls it in, wouldn't the waters leave the shore, making low tide rather than high tide?

Stanza 16. If the people referred to here were prehistoric, how do we know they prayed to the moon?

Stanza 18. Very nice, just right.

It would be wonderful to have a new book of yours on our list, and I think Hello, Harvest Moon *could become a fine counterpart to* Twilight Comes Twice. *I'd be glad to offer a contract if you are interested in working with me on a revision. It seems important to me that we be on the same wave-length before making a commitment. I look forward to hearing from you.*

My first reaction to this letter wasn't so much *hmm* as—*ouch!* Yes, it was a thoughtful letter. My editor had read my manuscript carefully. No doubt those comments and suggestions were meant to be helpful; instead they made me feel angry and "dissed." I felt like all the wind had been taken out of my sails.

At that point I no longer wanted to work on this book—I had lost my appetite—so I put the manuscript into a drawer. At times a writer needs to step away from the manuscript, and that's what I did now. I tried to calm down. Luckily, I had another writing project tugging at my sleeve, so I got busy with it.

Six weeks later Marian Reiner, my literary agent, phoned me.

"You should go back and take another look at that manuscript," she said. "It needs some work, sure, but I think she liked what you did."

"No, she didn't," I muttered.

"Yes, she did," Marian insisted. "Trust me: she wouldn't have spent so much time on it if she didn't believe that it had potential. Go back and take another look."

"Well, okay." Reluctantly I opened the drawer and pulled out the manuscript.

The first thing I did was to reread the manuscript. I did this several times. It was like trying to remember how to play or sing a favorite song. After receiving that letter from my editor, I had come to worry that my story was broken, fatally flawed. I needed to fall back in love with my story. Or, to put it another way, I had to reclaim the magic, to get back in touch with what had drawn me to write about the harvest moon in the first place.

My editor had *lots* of ideas for how I might strengthen this piece of writing. But how should I deal with them? If I looked at it as her telling me what to do, well, that dog wouldn't hunt, as my uncle used to say. In that case I would feel resistant, dig in my heels.

Here's what I learned from author Don Murray: *In this situation, the trick is to somehow make her suggestions my own.* Instead of thinking of it as her telling me what I should do, it would be more helpful to use her suggestions as a way to take a fresh look at (to re-vision) what I had written. Her ideas were not imperial decrees hurled down like lightning bolts from Mount Olympus; they were simply ideas she wanted me to consider. I knew that in the end I would use some of her ideas; others I would discard.

So I started another draft. As I wrote, I tried not to refer back to the original because I didn't want to be too tied to what I had written the first time around. It took me about two weeks to write it. When I finished, I sent it back to my editor. She liked what I had done. She wrote me another letter, shorter this time, with a few more suggestions.

For the next two months, we went back and forth like that. I would write a new draft; she would respond to it. It was like a friendly tug-of-war. Although I am not an illustrator, I pictured a lone wolf standing on a cliff, crying to the moon, so I kept including a stanza about the wolf. My editor would not budge on that ("Wolves are social creatures," she insisted) but she did accept other things I wanted to include (the luna moths, for example).

I signed a contract for *Hello, Harvest Moon.* The publisher assigned an illustrator, Kate Kiesler, who had also created the images for *Twilight Comes Twice.* Kate made a "dummy," a mockup with sketches, showing what text would appear on which pages.

On the next pages is the final, published manuscript.

The illustrator's mockup

Hello, Harvest Moon *(Final Draft)*

The crops have been gathered.
The pumpkins have been picked.
The silos are filled to bursting
with a million ears of corn.
Tired farmers are sound asleep.

But something is stirring
at the edge of the world.
Something is rising
low in the trees.

It comes up round, ripe and huge
over autumn fields of corn and wheat.
Hello, harvest moon.

With silent slippers
it climbs the night stairs,
lifting free of the treetops
to start working its magic,
staining earth and sky with a ghostly glow.

Harvest moonlight brushes your face,
makes you stir and blink, wake and wonder,
"Who left on that outside light?"

What radiance is streaming into your room!
It's so bright, you can read your favorite book
without even turning on the light.

Outside, the yards and streets seem to be
covered by a sparkling tablecloth.
Birch trees shine as if they have been
double-dipped
    in moonlight.

If you're lucky, you might spy
a few large luna moths
performing their ballet
in the crisp, cool air.

A garden spider builds her web,
hoping to catch an insect
drawn to the great lamp
in the sky.

Milkweed pods have cracked open,
spilling out spores
like tiny moonlights
        floating
                up to their mother.

If you played a nocturnal game of hide-and-seek
and hid behind that huge pine tree,
you would be almost invisible,
cloaked in moonshadow.

Now it's bedtime—but not for everyone.
Overhead a lone pilot is wide awake,
looking down, muttering to herself:
With all this moonshine, it's like
flying in broad daylight!

A night watchman gets out of his bed,
pulling on his boots, filling his thermos.
He always packs his flashlight,
though he wonders if he'll need it,
going to work on a night like this.

The harvest moon has its own work to do.
It paints the wings of owls and nighthawks
with a mixture of silver and shadow.

It speaks to the moonflower
Now! Now!
and sweet white blossoms unfold
though only night creatures
will see them.

It whispers to geese
Away! Away!
and they become restless
to start the long flight south.

Baby turtles emerge from eggs
tucked beneath the blanket of sand
where their mother left them
two months ago.
They make a mad dash to the ocean.

The harvest moon moves the earth's waters.
Grabbing whole oceans with its arms,
it pulls in the high tide
that will lift all the boats,
  every rowboat and yacht,
    tied snug at the dock.

It floods the clam flats with lonely lunar light,
setting off an eruption of bubbles
from clams and crabs
tucked in mud.

It floods us with dreams and memories
of every full moon we have ever seen.
It connects us to our distant ancestors
who prayed to the harvest moon
yet feared it might be a god's
one unblinking eye.

Finally it starts to ease lower . . .

. . . sprinkling silver coins
like a careless millionaire
over ponds, lakes, and seas,
till all the money is spent.

When you wake up,
look to the western horizon
and you might catch the moonset:
a sleepy head
  winking
    falling
      slow motion
        onto its pillow.
Goodnight, harvest moon.

Reflections on Writing *Hello, Harvest Moon*

So that is the journey, from beginning to end. What started with me looking up at the full moon on Halloween night eventually became a published book. The book certainly changed a great deal during the entire process. As I look back on this process, several things stand out.

- My notebook played an important role for me, especially at the beginning, by giving me a safe, private place where I could begin gathering and playing with material for the book. Forty gallons of maple sap must be boiled down to make one gallon of syrup. In a similar way, it took dozens of notebook pages to make this book.

- Although my editor's response made me angry at first, in the end it was helpful. It wasn't always a smooth ride, but I do believe she helped me to write a better book than I could have written without her.

- Some of the strongest lines (for example, "Birch trees shine as if they have been double-dipped in moonlight.") did not appear in the first draft. Sometimes when you revise, it's not enough just to tinker with a line you have written. *Sometimes you have to write new and better stuff.*

- Two of my favorite parts (the baseball image and the part about astronaut Neil Armstrong) got axed and don't appear in the published book. That's tragic, right? Well, yes and no. Even though those two stanzas got cut, I know that I can still use them in another piece of writing, perhaps a poem or another picture book. Writers are world-class recyclers. Nothing is ever truly lost.

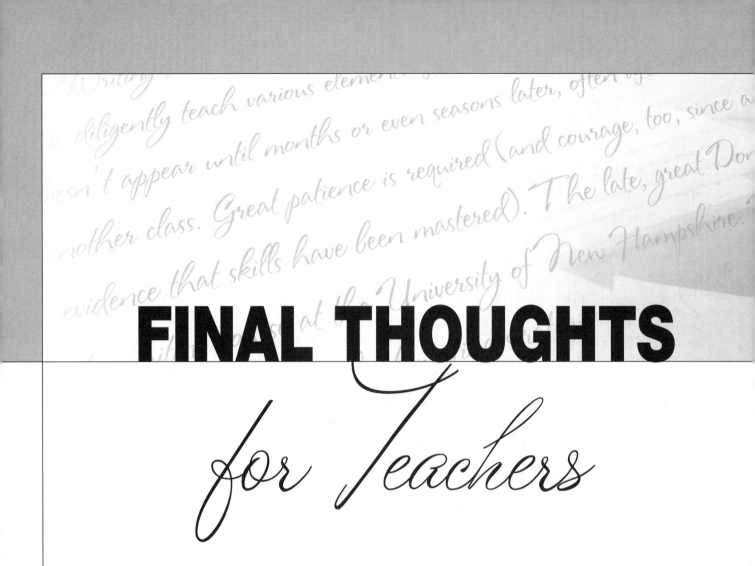

FINAL THOUGHTS
for Teachers

One teacher I know read to her third graders *17 Things I'm Not Allowed to Do Anymore* (2007), a picture book written by Jenny Offill and illustrated by Nancy Carpenter. Her students really liked this book, so much so that many were inspired to write their own versions. One boy wrote a comic book that included the page shown on the opposite page.

What happened here? This book certainly injected a jolt of energy into the writing workshop. It gave students a vision for a narrative structure they probably had never imagined. But did this book function as a mentor text, one that significantly lifted their writing? Did the students make true reading-writing connections, or did they merely borrow the *I'm not allowed* format and apply it to their own writing?

When my son Joseph was in eighth grade, he had Linda Rief (author of *101 Quickwrites* [2003]) as his language arts teacher. The two had a somewhat rocky relationship, though Linda did introduce Joseph to one piece of writing that made a strong impression on him. The poem was "Where I'm From," by George Ella Lyons (1999; see the appendix), a poem that has been widely used in language arts

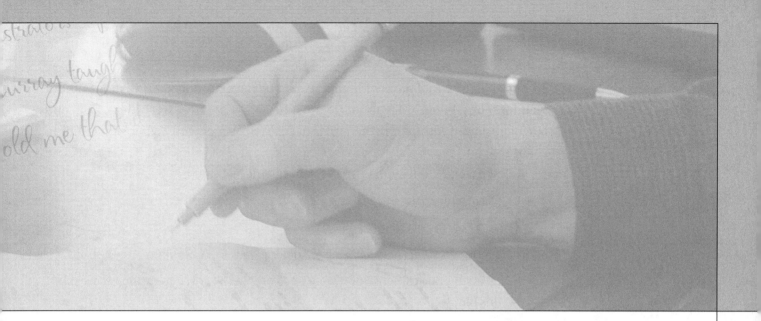

classrooms. Linda asked her students to read it several times.

"Where are you from?" she asked. Linda challenged them to write their own versions of this piece. Here's what Joseph wrote, in part:

> *I'm from Halloween, my all-time favorite holiday. I'm from our front porch, all decked out with spider webs, the severed head on a post and gory, disturbing decorations. I'm from the red strobe light and the fog machine that activates when the few little children who have the guts to do it come down the driveway.*
>
> *I'm from unbaked brownie batter, and the sick but satisfying feeling we get when Jake and I are done eating the whole bowl.*
>
> *I'm from my friends, from the tree house, from the Ping-Pong table in the barn, and the hammy we used as a zip-line handle to swing from one tree to another.*
>
> *I'm from my "Puff": my very-small-now but just-right-back-then blanket that I would take everywhere with me when I was very young.*

Joseph's writing impressed me. I admired the specificity as well as the tenderness. It's clear that Joseph's memoir and George Ella Lyons' poem are as connected as mother to infant son; you can practically see the umbilical cord between the two. By standing on the shoulders of Lyons' poem, Joseph was able to reach higher ground than he could have without it. Could he have produced his writing without reading Lyons' poem? Maybe so. He must have had the necessary ideas, skill, and language buried within him, but it took a close encounter with "Where I'm From" to coax them out.

What exactly did Joseph borrow from the original poem?

- use of a recurring line
- use of earthy details
- a tone of reminiscence, nostalgia, looking back
- the metaphorical sense of "where I'm from" (as opposed to the literal use of this phrase)

Joseph needed to deeply understand Lyons' poem in order to write his own version. It's worth noting that the word *understand* literally means to "stand under." Like a young plant beneath a powerful grow light, Joseph stood under Lyons' poem; his writing flourished in its glow. That is the magic that can take place when students apprentice themselves to an author they can springboard off to reach new heights in their own. Let me leave you with three final thoughts.

Open Source

Earlier, I borrowed this computer term to suggest a more democratic way for kids to enter into the life of a mentor text on their own terms, without undue guidance from teachers. But there's another way to think of it. Open source also means making sure your students venture beyond the safety of this book. Though it pains me to admit it ☺, there are plenty of other writers your students can apprentice themselves to! Encourage them to find other authors and texts they can learn from.

The Vision Thing

In her book *Study Driven*, Katie Ray (2006) explores the various ways powerful texts can give vision, a wider sense of possibility, to young writers. She writes:

> *I think it's worth asking, "Have I done enough to help my students develop a strong sense of vision for the writing I'd like them to do?" Writers write well, often even in first drafts, when they have a clear vision of the kind of writing they will do. (30)*

It's tempting to look at Joseph's writing as an example of a mentor text used in its truest sense, and the *I'm not allowed* example as more cursory and superficial. In fact, I believe that both mentor texts were instrumental in building vision in these writers. In each case, the student absorbed vision from the text, and used it to lift his writing. And each did so in a way that was appropriate to his level of development.

It's my hope that this book will help your students build vision, not just for a sense of the particular genre, but the wider vision for what constitutes strong writing. This "writing vision" is really what I'm after, and I believe it cuts across all genres.

Slow Growth

Let's remember that young writers grow slowly, and their development takes a great deal of time. Consider the difference between teaching craft elements in writing and teaching a concept in math. Typically we might introduce a math concept on Monday by modeling it for our students. We give homework exercises so kids can start to get comfortable with it. We check off the homework. Later in the week we might give students a quiz or pretest. The test on Friday gives solid data as to which students have mastered the concept, and which have not.

By contrast, writing is slow growth all the way. I adore blackberries, and so I was thrilled when last year wild blackberries spread through the meadow in my back yard. When I went forth in late July to harvest them, I was dismayed to find only thorny briars. I couldn't find a single berry. I despaired, and wondered if this was some rare fruitless variety.

This spring, a full year later, I was thrilled to see the same stalks produce white blossoms, which gave way to small green berries that will ripen in a few weeks. I hadn't known that this variety of blackberry takes two years to bear fruit.

Writing teachers, too, deal with a built-in time delay, which can be exasperating. We diligently teach various elements of the writer's craft, but the fruit of our labors often doesn't appear until months or even seasons later, often after the students have moved on to another class. Great patience is required (and courage, too, since administrators expect to see evidence that skills have been mastered). The late, great Don Murray taught a two-semester writing course at the University of New Hampshire. He told me that it was rare for his college students to absorb writing strategies immediately.

"I taught various writing strategies in the first semester, but usually my students didn't use those strategies in their writing until the spring semester."

My first published short story, "Tree Planting," was about a day I spent with an eighty-year-old doctor. We worked together planting baby trees in New Hampshire. The saplings were little bitty things, no more than six or eight inches tall.

"It'll take twenty years before they're even close to maturity," he admitted with a wry smile. "Guess I won't be around to see it."

We diligently teach the writer's craft, but the fruit of our labors often doesn't appear until months or seasons later...

I was struck by the quiet heroism of this act, planting trees that would never bring him shade. As writing teachers, we do the same thing. We share powerful texts that will give students new horizons for their writing. It won't happen today. It may not even happen this year, or next. But you can count on it: one day our young writers will blossom, even if we're not there when it happens. Except I actually think we will be there, buried deep inside them.

The End

References

Fletcher, Ralph. 1995. *Fig Pudding*. New York: Clarion Books.

———. 1997. *Ordinary Things: Poems from a Walk in Early Spring*. New York: Atheneum.

———. 1997. *Spider Boy*. New York: Clarion Books.

———. 1997. *Twilight Comes Twice*. New York: Clarion Books.

———. 1999. *Relatively Speaking: Poems About Family*. New York: Orchards Books.

———. 2001. *Uncle Daddy*. New York: Henry Holt.

———. 2003. *Hello, Harvest Moon*. New York: Clarion Books.

———. 2005. *A Writing Kind of Day*. Honesdale, PA: Boyds Mills Press.

———. 2011. *Also Known as Rowan Pohi*. New York: Clarion Books.

Ford, Richard. 1996. *The Sportswriter*. New York: Alfred A. Knopf.

Gantos, Jack. 2005. "The Follower." *Guys Read: Funny Business*. Edited by Jon Scieszka. New York: Viking.

Irving, John. 2000. *The World According to Garp*. New York: Random House.

Lyons, George Ella. 1999. *Where I'm From: Where Poems Come From*. Spring, TX: Absey & Company.

Nye, Naomi Shihab. 1990. "Valentine for Ernest Mann." In *The Place My Words Are Looking For*. New York: Bradbury Press.

Offill, Jenny. 2007. *17 Things I'm Not Allowed to Do Anymore*. New York: Schwartz and Wade Books.

Ray, Katie Wood. 2006. *Study Driven: A Framework for Planning Units of Study in the Writing Workshop*. Portsmouth, NH: Heinemann.

Reif, Linda. 2003. *101 Quickwrites: Fast and Effective Freewriting Exercises That Build Students' Confidence, Develop Their Fluency, and Bring Out the Writer in Every Student*. New York: Scholastic.

Yolen, Jane. 1987. *Owl Moon*. New York: Philomel.

Is there only one way to appro...

what they notice while reading my texts, you (teachers) will vary

feel is best for your unique group of students. To offer some ideas,

they would use th

Suggested Uses for
Mentor Author, Mentor Texts

in the Classroom

Is there only one way to approach this book? Of course not. Just as students will vary in what they notice while reading my texts, teachers who read this book will vary in which approach they feel is best for their unique group of students. To offer some ideas, I shared a draft of this book with educators from around the United States, inviting them to try it out with their students. Later, I asked them how they used it in their classrooms. Here's what they had to say.

These approaches could work no matter what level of experience your students have with mentor texts.

APPROACH	DESCRIPTION
Studying revision	Use the mentor texts to talk about revision. Connect the techniques used to students' own revision processes.

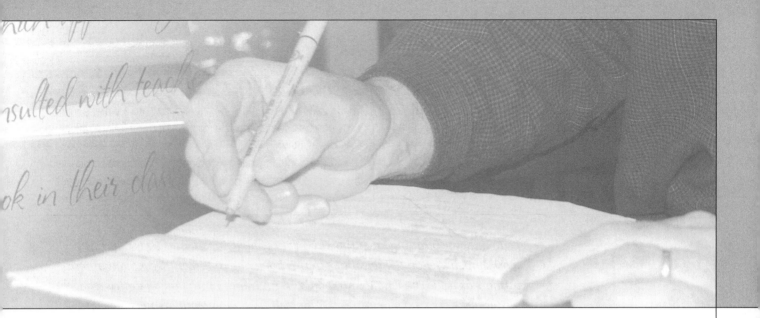

Ralph's four revision pieces are particularly helpful for students. Most of the time, students see revision as changing one word here or there, changing a lead, or omitting an extra word. Ralph's revisions are significant! How refreshing and challenging for students. His perspective on the painful, yet rewarding aspects of revision gives students a one-of-a-kind look at the powerful and important decisions writers make.

—Suzanne Whaley, Literacy Collaborative Coordinator at Bailey's
Elementary School for the Arts and Sciences in Fairfax County, Virginia

I would use particularly the last four pieces within a unit of study on revision. Since Ralph reveals his revision process and since readers can see both an early and finished draft, examining these pieces would be really instructive.

—Zoë Ryder White, tutor, grades K–6, Brooklyn, New York

APPROACH	DESCRIPTION
Student resource	Keep the book in your classroom as a student resource.

I would have a copy or two of the book available and accessible to students so that they can get it and use it as a resource during writing workshop.

—Zoë Ryder White

APPROACH	DESCRIPTION
Writer's notebooks and writing workshop	These texts and the notes give a window into a writer's mind. They can be used as models for how students might reflect on their own writing in their writer's notebooks, which can then be used as artifacts in writing workshops. They can also be used as a source of inspiration for thinking about how to use craft elements in students' own writing during writing workshops.

I can imagine building an entire unit of study on using mentor texts in writing workshop, based on the selections in this book and on other pieces from other authors as well. The whole unit would be an inquiry into how to notice what writers are doing, how to mine texts for techniques to try out on one's own, etc.

—Zoë Ryder White

I will use this book at the beginning of the year when I am setting the tone and systems and structures of writer's workshop, to experiment with a variety of genres for the first few weeks before we dig deep into individual genre studies.

—Sam Bennett, instructional coach, K–12, Denver, Colorado

This book is a perfect model of how writers in the world collect their thoughts. A writer's notebook has quotes, beliefs, short and extended pieces of writing and reflection. I will use Ralph's book as a model for students to collect their written work and their thinking and reflection on that work over time as evidence of growth throughout the year. Each set of writer's notes offers a model of where ideas come from, reflection, goal setting, and revision. The book illuminates again and again the idea that words just don't "arrive," they are crafted. Writing doesn't just "capture" thinking, it is thinking.

—Sam Bennett

These approaches might be valuable if you have never used mentor texts in your classroom and are just testing the waters of talking about craft, style, tone, and other writing elements.

APPROACH	DESCRIPTION
Whole-class discussion	Use a document camera or SMART Board to project a mentor text for all to see together. Together, discuss and explore the text and the writer's thinking behind it.

When we study a piece as a class, we project the text using a document camera or SMART Board. First, students are encouraged to write down what they notice about the author's craft in their writer's notebook during a five-minute reflection. Next, students turn and talk with a partner about what tricks Ralph used in his piece. (My kids love talking about writing in terms of "tricks" because they are familiar with "tricks" in video games.) This partner-share gives each student the opportunity to be heard and to practice talking about writing. Most of my students do not have experience talking about writer's craft, so inviting them to discuss craft helps them to think and live like writers. Finally, we share what we noticed as a whole class and students record their observations on either the projected piece or the SMART Board. When we are done, we have a piece of writing that has been unpacked as a class. One advantage to talking about the passage as a class is that we create a shared experience that we can refer to and draw upon later. Developing these common reference points gives the students material to refer back to during peer revision conferences and writer's share.

—Kate Norem Morris, classrom teacher, The Bush School, Seattle, Washington

APPROACH	DESCRIPTION
Structured small-group discussions	Read a mentor text aloud; ask students to talk in small groups to gather thoughts and observations; talk as a whole class to build on the small groups' thinking.

In any given week if you were to peek into my classroom and watch as we used this resource, the first thing you would see is my students gathered around me on the carpet eager to hear texts brought to life. They know that the first time we read one of Ralph's texts it is simply an opportunity for us to savor the story and allow language to linger in our heads and hearts. This is one of the most crucial parts of the process, because my students are more open to learning from a text if they have a relationship with it. Another reason I read aloud to my students this first time is that it gives all of my students an entry point for the passage, even those who would struggle with reading it independently. After my kids have heard the passage read aloud, I give them an opportunity to talk about it with a partner. Since more than 60 percent of my students are English language learners, it is important that they have a chance to discuss the text in a low-risk situation, such as turn and talk, before we break out and talk about our ideas as a whole class. During this initial introduction, my students focus on the content of the piece, rather than the *craft. They wonder about and wrestle with the passage's ideas. I have found that it is better if I let the passage settle with my students for a day before diving into discussing the writer's craft.*

—Kate Norem Morris

These approaches might be valuable if you have used mentor texts occasionally in your classroom and many of your students engage in conversations about craft, style, tone, and other elements of writing.

APPROACH	DESCRIPTION
Independent small-group discussions	Ask students to work in small groups to read and talk about a text and the writing techniques in it.

When we unpack a passage in teams, students work in groups of three to record what they find most intriguing or compelling. Students are given a copy of the piece we are reading, along with the writer's notes, and gather in nooks around the room to unlock the magic of the piece. Often students record what they notice both in their notebooks and on the actual copy of the text. When we are done, students hang their marked-up texts on a section of our classroom wall called The Garage. This section of our room is named The Garage because it is where we learn about how writing works, just like a garage for cars is where a mechanic learns about how cars work. Once the writing is hung in The Garage, students can choose to read over what other teams noticed or to simply focus on what they noticed in their team.

—Kate Norem Morris

APPROACH	DESCRIPTION
Charting writing techniques	Use a chart to develop insights into and a working language of ways writers create specific effects in readers. This helps students develop a wider repertoire of writing techniques.

One way to explicitly connect students' reactions with the specific techniques to writing is to record our thinking by creating a class chart. We post the chart to our Writers' Toolbox wall so that we can return to this co-constructed learning. Here's a chart we made after reading "Interview with a Coho Salmon."

—Suzanne Whaley, Literacy Collaborative Coordinator at Bailey's
Elementary School for the Arts and Sciences in Fairfax County, Virginia

GENERAL REACTIONS	HOW THE WRITER DID IT	WHAT IT DOES FOR THE READER
"It's funny."	Included puns and jokes	Keeps the reader interested, especially when reading lots of facts in nonfiction
"The salmon talks!"	Personified the salmon by making her a "character"	Helps the reader connect and empathize with the amazing life of all salmon by focusing on one salmon
"There are some hard words in there."	Included specialized vocabulary about the topic	Teaches the reader new or technical words in the context of the whole

APPROACH	DESCRIPTION
Conferring and creating minilessons	Use mentor texts to talk about ways particular writers have worked through particular writing situations. Try this in individual writing conferences or with the whole class through a lesson or minilesson.

One of my students, Suzy, knows that she struggles to provide enough detail in her nonfiction pieces and has been working on this goal for several months. When we met for a writing conference on her piece about soccer, she told me that she knew she needed to include more details because her reader might not know anything about soccer and she didn't want the reader to be confused. At this point in the year, we had already read Ralph's piece "Squirming Wizards of Recycling," so Suzy and I pulled it out and looked at the writer's notes. In the notes, Ralph said he had brainstormed questions that readers may have had as they read about worm composting and he then tried to include the answers to those questions in the piece. Suzy decided that she would write down questions that she thought her reader might still have about soccer and then make sure those questions were answered in her writing. Since both Suzy and I have already developed a relationship with Ralph through his texts, it felt like we were inviting an old friend to join our conference.

—Kate Norem Morris

This book can be used as a personal teaching resource. I might copy a piece for the whole group to study as they see fit, as an idea comes up. For example, my kids could use some help with revision and with using metaphor, and many of Ralph's texts are great examples of these techniques. I would also use these texts in minilessons.

—Zoë Ryder White

APPROACH	DESCRIPTION
Think-alouds	Use the "Writer's Notes" sections as models for students to "think aloud" about their own writing processes and the decisions they make as writers.

This book is a great model for "think-alouds." The text is a powerful example of how a writer thinks. For teachers who struggle doing "write-alouds" with students, this book offers a terrific model and will inspire them to give their own writing a go.

—Sam Bennett, instructional coach, K–12, Denver, Colorado

These approaches might be valuable if you use mentor texts regularly in your classroom and your students frequently engage in conversations about craft, style, tone, and other writing techniques.

APPROACH	DESCRIPTION
Studying a specific technique	Study a specific craft element, such as metaphor, and the ways it affects the writing and the reader.

I occasionally use some of these pieces with a whole group when I'm pretty confident that the whole group will connect to a piece, and the writer's notes will bring out a key point that would benefit most of the students in the class. For example, "Quilt," "Sibling Blanketry," and "Driving at Night" are pieces with strong metaphors that students often respond to. Most students benefit from learning from Ralph's thinking when using metaphor in narrative pieces.

—Suzanne Whaley, Literacy Collaborative Coordinator at Bailey's
Elementary School for the Arts and Sciences in Fairfax County, Virginia

I pull a small group working on nonfiction to look closely at "Squirming Wizards of Recycling" or "Interview with a Coho Salmon." Sometimes the students are struck by the personification of the salmon. Other times they're struck by Ralph's voice in "Squirming Wizards of Recycling." In either case, it's my job as the teacher to explicitly show them how they can purposefully take on these new techniques in their own writing.

—Suzanne Whaley

APPROACH	DESCRIPTION
Studying a particular genre	Study a specific genre, such as poetry, to learn more about creating texts in that genre.

A great use for this book is to take relevant texts within genre-based units of study. For example, collect all of the poems for use within a poetry unit and organize them by a particular craft move, such as circular structure, and then students can look at a specific poem that shows this.

—Zoë Ryder White

APPROACH	DESCRIPTION
Studying a variety of texts in small groups	Create stations or centers in the classroom; place a different mentor text at each station and ask students to rotate through all the texts, adding to their repertoire with each reading.

I make multiple copies of pieces from this book and create reading stations. I ask my students—in groups of pairs and triads—to find a station and read the mentor text at that station just for the pure enjoyment of the text. Then I have them reread the text, thinking about the suggested questions (see page xiv). After their discussion, each group finds another group in the class who has read the same text. This time they read the text knowing their discussion will revolve around how the piece was written. Students who read the same texts meet together to share their thoughts.

—Paul Crivelli, fifth-grade teacher at Increase Miller Elementary School in
    Goldens Bridge, New York

APPROACH	DESCRIPTION
"Let's not talk, let's think."	Support students in engaging with the texts individually.

On days when my students turn to mentor texts independently, I give them each a photocopy of both the text and the writer's notes that is small enough for them to glue or staple into their writer's notebook. I then invite them to breathe in the pieces, to be inspired by them. One reason I really like this format is that it allows students to interact with the text at their own pace. I can think of one student, Jesus, who tends to spend less than five minutes on his reflection, then chooses a technique from the piece and immediately tries it on in his own writing. In the same class, Kendy spends her entire writing time recopying the passage onto a blank piece of her notebook with notes carefully written in the margin about what she notices in the text.

—Kate Norem Morris

APPROACH	DESCRIPTION
"What would Ralph do?": Channeling a mentor author	After studying many texts by the same author, teach students to call on their knowledge of that writer. In a particular writing situation, they can ask themselves, "What would Ralph do here?" and try that in their writing. This will give them another tool to address those tough decisions they must make as writers.

Using this resource has allowed our class to partner with Ralph on a daily basis. Just as I am sure they do in classes all across the country, my students often stop to wonder, "What would Ralph do here?" But their curiosity about craft has spilled over beyond questions about Ralph's writing and has inspired my students to wonder about every author's difficult decisions, techniques, and tricks.

—Kate Norem Morris

APPROACH	DESCRIPTION
Student-led inquiry	Support students in choosing their text and their reading or writing approach based on their own writing needs.

One use for this book is to copy a variety of pieces in a packet for students and have them choose the one piece that speaks to them the most strongly/clearly, and somehow present (in writing, out loud) their reactions to that piece—why they are drawn to it, what they admire about it, etc., and then have them try out one thing in their own writing that they learned from that piece.

—Zoë Ryder White

Conclusion

While all of these ideas should help you find entry points into ways to incorporate these texts into your students' daily writing lives, many teachers have also found that this book can be used as a tool for their own professional development. You might consider using these mentor texts in teacher study groups, where you study the writer's craft together and then consider how to bring that learning about craft back to your students. Here is one educator's idea of how to use this book for professional development.

I think this book is a great resource to use for teacher study groups and for professional development for teachers who want to develop their own craft as writers. It is a great resource for different teacher Writing Projects across the country. Ralph's introductory piece ["Contagious Magic"] functions as a This I Believe essay, the why behind the reasons to read and write, instead of a focus on the what. He makes a compelling case and this can be used as a great model for teachers to reflect on what they believe matters most to help students grow in their writing craft.

—Sam Bennett

Keep the mentoring going
with more of Ralph Fletcher's treasured resources

Professional Books

Writing Workshop: *The Essential Guide*
Ralph Fletcher and JoAnn Portalupi provide everything a teacher needs to get a writing workshop up and running well.

978-0-325-00362-7 / 2001 / 176pp

What a Writer Needs
Ralph provides practical strategies for challenging and extending student writing during workshop with specifics on teaching the elements of craft.

978-0-435-08734-0 / 1992 / 192pp

Breathing In, Breathing Out: *Keeping a Writer's Notebook*
Ralph focuses on the writer's notebook, examining what it is, how writers—especially students—can use it, and why published writers consider their notebooks invaluable.

978-0-435-07227-8 / 1996 / 112pp

Classroom Resources from *first*hand

Teaching the Qualities of Writing
JoAnn and Ralph's hands-on lessons explore ideas, design, language, and presentation, showing how to infuse each with voice to energize students' writing.

978-0-325-00629-1 / 2004 / 112 Lesson Cards + Teaching Guide + CD-ROM

Lessons for the Writer's Notebook
Ralph and JoAnn provides a series of lessons that introduce the writer's notebook, sustain it, and transition writers from notebooks to finished pieces.

978-0-325-00912-4 / 2006 / 20 Lesson Cards + Teaching Guide + Audio CD

CALL **800.225.5800** FAX **877.231.6980** VISIT **Heinemann.com** DEDICATED TO TEACHERS